COLLINS GEM GUIDES

WILD ANIMALS

illustration by
Bruce Pearson

text by
John A. Burton

First published 1980

© illustrations Bruce Pearson and
text John A. Burton 1980

ISBN 0 00 458802 9

Colour reproduction by Adroit Photo-Litho Ltd, Birmingham

Filmset by Jolly & Barber Ltd, Rugby

Printed and bound by Wm Collins Sons and Co Ltd, Glasgow

Reprint 20 19 18 17 16 15 14 13 12 11

Contents

How to Use this Book

This guide describes and illustrates most of the mammals found in Europe. A few are not illustrated, as they look virtually identical to closely related species, or are so rare that they are only likely to be found by an expert.

The book has two primary functions. First, it is a general background to European mammals, enabling the reader to become acquainted with their general appearance, distribution and characteristics. Second, being a convenient, pocket-sized book, it can be used as an identification aid in the field. It is not, however, meant to identify all species, and it must be emphasised that certain groups of small mammals, such as rodents, shrews and bats, can be extremely difficult to identify. It should be possible to identify from this book most of the larger species, but with smaller species the aim is to give only a broad guide.

Measurements

For each species an overall length for adults has been given. This body length normally includes the head, but not the tail unless otherwise stated. Other measurements, such as shoulder height (for deer etc.) and weights, are also given where appropriate. All measurements are intended only as an approximate guide.

Names
All the mammals have been given vernacular names, where possible the most common ones. Alternatives for these are in brackets, and synonyms of the scientific names are also given where appropriate.

Distribution
For simplicity some rather loose geographical terms have been used, e.g. Iberia refers to the Iberian peninsula; Scandinavia generally excludes Denmark; and the Balkans refers to Yugoslavia, Romania, Hungary, Bulgaria, Greece and Albania. Descriptions of distribution are intended only as an approximate guide.

Further Reading
Readers wanting further information should consult some of the following: M. Burton, *Guide to the Mammals of Britain and Europe* (Elsevier/Phaidon, 1976); R. Burton, *Carnivores of Europe* (Batsford, 1979); G. B. Corbet, *The Mammals of the Palearctic Region, A Taxonomic Review* (British Museum (Natural History), 1978); G. B. Corbet, *The Terrestrial Mammals of Western Europe* (Foulis, 1966); G. B. Corbet and D. Ovenden, *The Mammals of Britain* (Collins, 1980); G. B. Corbet and H. N. Southern (ed.), *The Handbook of British Mammals* (Blackwell, 1977); P. G. H. Evans, 'Cetaceans in British Waters', *Mammal Review*, vol. 10, no. 1 (1980); D. Ovenden, G. B. Corbet and E. N. Arnold, *Collins Handguide to the Wild Animals of Europe* (Collins, 1979); F. J. Taylor Page, *Field Guide to British Deer* (Blackwell, 1971).

Introduction

One of the first things to be borne in mind when you go into the field in Europe looking for wild mammals is that you are unlikely to see many. After centuries of persecution most of the larger mammals have either been exterminated or are very shy, and most mammals, in order to avoid man and other predators, are nocturnal. It is therefore equally important to look out for signs and remains indicating the presence of mammals, such as footprints, food remains and nests. These have been described where relevant.

Mammal Habitats

Mammals are found in nearly all parts of Europe, except the bleakest, and the topmost parts of mountains. By knowing what to expect, and the signs to look for in any particular environment, you can greatly increase your chance of seeing a mammal.

Deciduous Woodland

Before man cleared it, much of Europe was covered by deciduous or mixed woodlands, and there were many more marshes. Deciduous woodlands (see p. 7) are still among the best habitats to look for mammals. Deer can be difficult to observe in woodland, but their footprints, droppings and other signs can often be found. In the dense undergrowth dormice and a variety of other rodents and insectivores excavate their tunnels and build nests. Fallen logs provide cover for the smaller species – but remember to replace any logs you move. Disused woodpecker holes and hollow trees provide roosting sites for a number of species of bats, and at dusk it should be possible to observe bats hawking for insects in the more open parts of the wood. In winter the dreys built by squirrels are often very obvious, though totally concealed during the summer months. Although rarely seen in woodlands, moles are often common, but their runs and hills are hidden beneath the leafy litter; similarly hares are rarely so obvious as when they are in open fields – yet they are also often common. Occasionally predators – such as Weasels, Stoats, Polecats or Foxes – may be glimpsed.

Farmland

Although farmland is a totally man-made habitat, because of its variety it can often provide a home for a wide variety of mammals. The farm buildings invariably harbour several species of rats and mice, and bats will roost in the roofs. Hedgerows, which are in effect miniature 'edge of woodland' habitats, provide one of the most diverse of all habitats and abound with mice, shrews, voles and dormice which in turn provide food for Weasels, Stoats, Foxes and other animals. Badgers often live in woods and copses near farmland, emerging at night to feed on worms in the pastures and meadows. Deer will also lie up in woodlands and come out to feed on the fields at night.

In addition much farmland has also been preserved for game hunting. This means that farmers will overlook some of the damage done by species such as deer, hares, boar and foxes in order to hunt them. However other species, such as weasels, stoats and even hedgehogs and rodents, may be persecuted relentlessly. Game preserving reached a peak at the beginning of this century, and many wild animals became rare at this time. In Britain the Wild Cat, Polecat and Pine Marten were almost exterminated. However changing attitudes in recent years, combined with the fact that farmers can no longer afford a large staff of gamekeepers, has meant that some of the rarer species are gradually increasing again.

But in the last quarter of a century a newer, more serious, threat has arisen: pollution. Modern farming uses vast amounts of chemicals to control insect pests; these often accumulate in other animals, eventually killing them too. Animals such as bats and Otters are believed to have become almost extinct in some areas as a direct result of the use of chemical pesticides.

Wetlands

The majority of Europe's once extensive wetlands have now been drained or reduced to tiny remnants of their former glory. Marshes, fens, estuaries and bogs are still regarded by many people as wastelands, and yet for wildlife they are among the richest habitats. The isolated fragments of wetlands that remain are now threatened with pollution, particularly rivers and lakes. Despite this many mammals are still to be found in wetlands. The banks of rivers and lakes, and logs and rocks jutting out into the water, are good places to look for the droppings and food remains of aquatic mammals such as Water voles, Beavers, Water shrews, Mink and Otters. The muddy edge of a river or lake may well show clear footprints. Several species of bat are found mainly in wetland areas and can be seen hawking for insects over the water in the evening or by moonlight; some bats even take insects and small fish from the surface of the water. Seals, particularly Common Seals, as well as dolphins and porpoises, may travel considerable distances up rivers, and in Finland Ringed Seals live in land-locked lakes (p. 162). Several of the exotic species of mammal introduced into Europe are likely to be encountered in wetland areas – the Coypu and Musk Rat are particularly aquatic, and the Raccoon, American Mink and Chinese Water Deer can all be found near water.

Coniferous Woods and Mountains
The mountains and northern Europe contain some of the least disturbed habitats, and it is in these last strongholds that a few of the larger animals that once roamed Europe can still be glimpsed. In the Alps, Pyrenees, Carpathians and a few other mountain areas, Marmots, Ibex and Chamois can be found, while in Scandinavia the Wolverine and Arctic Fox, Reindeer, Wolf and Lynx still survive – but only just. Interesting species such as the all-black Alpine Shrew and the long-haired Snow Vole are also found.

Other Habitats
There are a number of other interesting habitats, which have their own particular mammal fauna – such as the steppes of eastern Europe, and the shores

and islands which provide shelter for seals. Before going into the field it is always worth checking which species are likely to be encountered in any particular habitat, as it will often help to know what to look for.

Conservation

Most of Europe's spectacular species have disappeared from all but remote corners of the continent. However there is increasing concern for rare and endangered species, and protective measures have been instigated in many countries. The reintroduction and translocation of lost species may well mean that, in the not too distant future, it will be possible to see animals outside the ranges described in this volume. Species involved include Ibex, Marmot, Mouflon, Beaver, Saiga, Bison and Lynx. However some, such as the Wolverine, Reindeer, Wolf and some bats, seem doomed to extinction unless adequate conservation measures are implemented. Several European countries have already published, or are preparing, 'Red Data Books' of threatened wildlife. Numerous national societies are working together with government agencies to conserve what is left of Europe's depleted mammalian fauna.

HEDGEHOGS

Northern
Hedgehog

young
newborn

The 3 species of hedgehog found in Europe are the **Northern Hedgehog** (*Erinaceus europaeus*) and the **Algerian** or **Vagrant Hedgehog** (*E. algirus*) and the **Eastern Hedgehog** (*E. concolor*). The Northern Hedgehog is widespread, and often common, over most of Europe, except the more northerly parts of Scandinavia, Finland and the USSR; it is also found on many islands and Eastern Europe where it is replaced by the pale throated Eastern species. The

$\times \frac{3}{4}$

fore

hind

Algerian Hedgehog has a very restricted range in Europe and is only found on the Mediterranean coasts of Spain and France and the Balearics; it is also found in North Africa. They are found in a wide variety of mainly wooded habitats and are often common in suburban gardens. Hedgehogs grow up to about 25cm long (the tail is largely concealed) and weigh between 800–1,400gm, depending on the time of year. Although unlikely to be confused with any other animals, the 3 species are very similar, but the Algerian Hedgehog has lighter spines and longer legs than the Northern Hedgehog and also a parting in the spines on its forehead.

Hedgehogs are mainly active in the twilight and at night. They are often very noisy and can run and climb, though the normal reaction to the onset of danger is to roll into a ball, erecting the spines at different angles and covering the underparts. Hedgehogs are mainly insectivorous. They make nests of leaves and grasses and 2–9 pink, soft-spined young are born in late spring or early summer and there is sometimes a second litter. They hibernate in winter.

**Algerian
Hedgehog**

SHREWS

Introduction

Shrews are small insectivorous mammals and include the world's smallest known mammals; they used to be known as Shrew-mice. One or more species are found in most parts of Europe except the permanently frozen areas of the extreme north and the tops of the higher mountains; they occur on most islands except the smaller ones. Although they are not often seen, their high-pitched squeaking can often be heard, and their remains are often found in the pellets of birds of prey (owls and hawks regurgitate the bones, fur and feathers of their prey), and they are occasionally found dead on paths, drowned or trapped in discarded bottles. For like other small mammals they enter bottles and, once inside, the slippery sloping neck prevents them pushing their way out and they die; the corpses often attract other mammals and accumulations of 20 or more have been found in a single bottle; indeed searching for

discarded bottles is often a good way of establishing what small mammals are present in an area. The most distinctive features of shrews are their long pointed snouts and small pointed teeth, characteristic of many insectivorous mammals such as hedgehogs, desmans and moles; the fur is often rather short and velvety.

The European shrews fall broadly into 3 groups: **Water shrews** *Neomys* species (p. 20) which are relatively large and have black fur above, and red-tipped teeth; **Red-toothed shrews** *Sorex* species (p. 18) which are smaller than *Neomys*, have red-tipped teeth and variably coloured fur; and **White-toothed shrews** *Crocidura* and *Suncus* species (p. 22) which lack pigmentation in their teeth and are rather variable in colour.

However, although size, tooth colour and range can often identify the more obvious species it is often necessary to consult specialist books to identify shrews positively.

RED-TOOTHED SHREWS

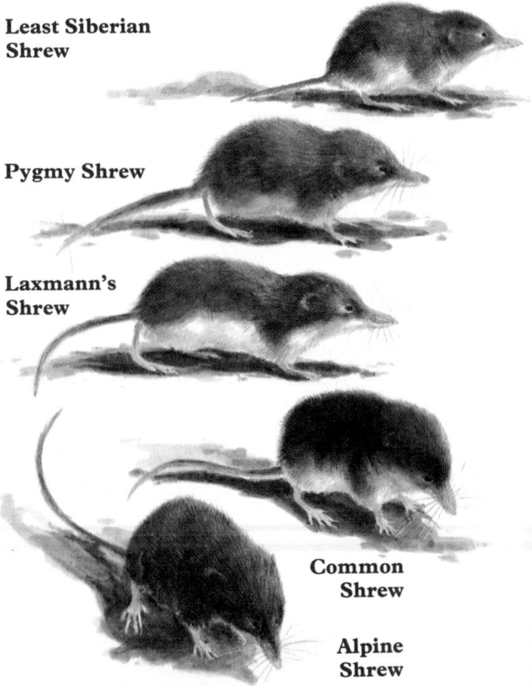

**Least Siberian
Shrew**

Pygmy Shrew

**Laxmann's
Shrew**

**Common
Shrew**

**Alpine
Shrew**

One or more of the 7 species of Red-toothed shrews are found over most of Europe but they are absent from most Mediterranean islands. The Pygmy and Common Shrews are the most widespread, being found from Britain and France eastwards; the Pygmy is also found in Ireland. Laxmann's or Masked Shrew is found in isolated pockets from Sweden and Poland eastwards, the Spanish in central Spain, the Alpine in the highlands of central Europe, the Pyrenees, Balkans, Carpathians and Tatras. The Least Siberian and Dusky Shrews are found in Scandinavia eastwards through Russia to Siberia. Although very similar, the following characteristics will help to identify the different species; the only other shrews with red tooth-tips are the Water shrews (p. 20).

The **Least Siberian Shrew** *Sorex minutissimus* is only found in the taiga zone of northern Europe; it is extremely small, less than 50mm plus a tail of less than 30mm. The **Pygmy Shrew** *S. minutus* is widespread and small, 45–60mm long plus a tail of up to 60mm. The **Common Shrew** *S. araneus* is also widespread, medium sized, 60–85mm plus a relatively short tail of up to 55mm, and dark above with paler flanks and pale undersides. The **Alpine Shrew** *S. alpinus* is only found in upland areas; it is largish, up to about 75mm plus a tail nearly the same length, and is a uniform dark colour. The **Spanish Shrew** *S. granarius*, the **Dusky Shrew** *S. sinalis (isodon)* and **Laxmann's Shrew** *S. caecutiens* can only be distinguished by an expert.

WATER SHREWS

dark
form

typical
form

**Northern
Water Shrew**

The 2 species of Water shrew found in Europe are
the **Northern Water Shrew** *Neomys fodiens* and
the **Southern Water Shrew** (also known as
Miller's Water Shrew) *N. anomalus*. The former
inhabits most of Europe including the far north but
is absent from much of Iberia, south-east Europe
and islands except Britain; it is usually found close to
water, particularly slow-moving streams, but also in
a variety of habitats. It is one of the largest shrews
and grows to a total length of up to 14cm of which the

tail is less than half; its fur is blackish above and sometimes black but usually white underneath, the teeth are red-tipped, the tail has a 'keel' of stiff hairs and the hind feet are fringed with hairs. The Southern Water Shrew is less tied to water than the Northern species but its range is restricted to the higher altitudes of Spain, France, and central Europe (as far south as northern Italy); however it is more widespread in eastern and south-east Europe. The 2 species are very similar in appearance but the Southern is always white below, lacks the stiff hairs on the tail and has less hair on the feet. Both species swim and dive well and appear silvery under water. They make a variety of squeaks, dig tunnels along the water's edge and are among the most easily observed of the shrews; they feed on a variety of insects, crustaceans and other invertebrates. Water shrews are most likely to be confused with moles (p. 26) which have enlarged fore-paws, or the Alpine Shrew (p. 18) which never has white on the underside and has a longer tail.

Southern Water Shrew

WHITE-TOOTHED SHREWS

Greater White-toothed Shrew

Lesser White-toothed Shrew

Pygmy White-toothed Shrew

The 4 species of white-toothed shrews are the **Lesser** *Crocidura suaveolens*, the **Greater** *C. russula*, the **Bicoloured** *C. leucodon* and the **Pygmy** (Savi's or Etruscan) **White-toothed Shrew** *Suncus etruscus*. They are widespread in southern, central and eastern Europe but only the Lesser White-toothed Shrew is found in Britain and then only in the Isles of Scilly. White-toothed shrews are found in a wide variety of fairly dry but well-vegetated habitats and it can be very difficult to separate the different species. The Lesser and the Greater are virtually indistinguishable although the Lesser grows to about 80mm plus a tail of up to 40mm, and the Greater to about 95mm plus a tail of up to 45mm. The Bicoloured is smaller and has a pale underside and contrasting darker upperparts. The Pygmy is the smallest known mammal, weighing less than 2gm and measuring up to 50mm in length plus a tail of up to 30mm; it has largish ears, reddish upperparts and is found at low altitudes. Apart from the problems of identifying the different species of White-toothed shrews, they may be confused with the Red-toothed shrews (p. 18) unless the teeth are examined.

Bicoloured
with young

DESMANS

The 2 species of desman found in Europe are the
Pyrenean Desman *Galemys pyrenaica* which inhabits fast-flowing mountain streams, with dense
vegetation along the banks, at an altitude of 300–
1,200m, in the Pyrenees, north-western Spain and
Portugal; and the **Russian Desman** *Desmana
moschata* which occurs in the river systems of the
Don and Volga and has been introduced into the
Dnepr. The Russian species is valued for its fur.

24

Desmans are best described as aquatic moles. They are among the most aquatic of all Europe's mammals and show a number of modifications for their life: the tail is slightly flattened and fringed with hairs; the feet are also fringed with hair and the hind feet are webbed; the nostrils have valves and open upwards on the long, mobile, spatulate snout which can be used as a snorkel; water repellent guard hairs protect the dense insulating underfur. The Pyrenean Desman grows up to 13.5cm plus a very long tail of up to 15.5cm and weighs up to 80gm; the Russian Desman is much larger – up to 45cm long. They can sometimes be observed walking under water and feed almost entirely on the beds of streams and rivers where they take mainly aquatic invertebrates, and occasionally small animals. A single litter of about 4 young is produced in spring or early summer. Within their restricted ranges desmans are often abundant but they are frequently overlooked as they are nocturnal. They are unlikely to be confused with any other species within their ranges.

Russian Desman
breathing
in water

25

MOLES

European Mole

There are 3 very closely related and very similar species of mole in Europe: the **European Mole** *Talpa europaea* is found in all parts except the Mediterranean zones and as far north as Britain and southern Sweden; the **Mediterranean** or **Blind Mole** *T. caeca* is generally found in the Mediterranean zones of Iberia, Italy and the Balkans; the **Roman Mole** *T. romana* is confined to southern Italy and Macedonia. All 3 are found mostly in wooded habitats wherever there is soil for burrowing. The only immediately obvious difference between the species is size: the Roman Mole is the largest, growing to a length of up to 16.5cm, the

Mediterranean Mole may be as small as 95mm and the European Mole is intermediate, measuring 11·5–14cm and weighing 65–120gm; however, there is considerable variation among species. In all 3 the eye is very small, and in the Mediterranean and Roman Moles the opening may not be visible; the snout and front legs are often whitish in the Mediterranean Mole. Moles spend most of their life tunnelling underground using the enlarged fore-paws to dig; these tunnels are often clearly visible, as are the molehills which are pushed up at intervals; the breeding chamber (fortress) is excavated beneath the ground. They feed mainly on earthworms. In very dry weather moles may be seen on the surface and might be confused with Water (p. 20) or Alpine (p. 18) shrews, both of which have long tails and lack the enlarged fore-paws.

Roman Mole

Mediterrean Mole

molehills

27

BATS

Introduction

Although bats are often the most frequently observed mammals in Europe they are among the most difficult to identify and are surprisingly little studied. Most species are virtually impossible to identify on the wing with any degree of certainty, though with the aid of electronic 'bat detectors', which reduce the high-frequency sounds emitted by bats to a pitch audible to humans, some can be identified. However, all species of bats sleep for most of the day, and in most parts of Europe hibernate during the winter months, and when hanging in their roosts they are a little easier to identify. However roosting bats are sensitive to disturbance and, since many species are known to be declining, it is best to disturb them as little as possible. With flying bats the type of features to look for are the height and speed at which they fly and the type of flight – do they hover, swoop or flutter. At closer quarters, the shape and size of the ears is an important aid to identification (the ears of some species can be seen in flight); in Horseshoe bats the muzzle and nose-piece should be studied. Other useful aids to identification are the size of the feet, coloration, habitat and roosting site. Bats can be attracted to bat boxes, which are like nest boxes provided for birds, but have a slit on the underside.

MYOTIS BATS

The **Whiskered Bat** *Myotis mystacinus*
and **Brandt's Whiskered Bat** *M. brandti*
are extremely similar and can only be
differentiated by an expert. Between them,
they are found in most of Europe including
Britain and Ireland. They are among the smallest
of European bats, with a body length of just over
40mm, and weigh under 10gm. They are found in
wooded areas and roost in trees, roofs, outbuildings
or cellars during the summer and in caves, mines,
cellars and, more rarely, hollow trees in winter. They
usually hide in cracks and crevices but emerge early
and sometimes fly by day. They are most likely to be
confused with other *Myotis* bats, which are all larger,
or the Pipistrelles (p. 38), which are smaller with
rounded ears.

Natterer's Bat *M. nattereri* is widespread over most of Europe, as far north as Britain and Ireland and southern Scandinavia, but absent from most of south-east Europe. It is on average slightly larger than the preceding species. Its most noticeable features are the fringe of hair on the edge of the tail membrane, its rather pale, pointed muzzle and fairly long ears.

The **Long-fingered Bat** *M. capacinii* is found in Italy, southern France, western Spain and various parts of south-eastern Europe; it is also found on several Mediterranean islands. Like the preceding species it usually inhabits fairly well-wooded habitats and it is often found near water. It is rather similar to Daubenton's Bat (p. 34), but slightly larger, having even larger hind feet with rather hairy shins. Like Daubenton's Bat it hunts mostly over water, often skimming the surface.

Natterer's Bat

Long-fingered Bat

MOUSE-EARED BATS

Large
Mouse-eared
Bat

Lesser
•Mouse-eared Bat

The **Large Mouse-eared Bat** *Myotis myotis* is widely distributed in central and southern Europe and is found on many Mediterranean islands; its range extends north to the English Channel, the Netherlands and the Baltic coast of Germany and there is a tiny population in England. In most of the northern parts of its range it is declining and is considered endangered in some countries and is protected in many (including Britain). It is found in a variety of habitats, often in towns, roosting throughout the year in cellars and mines, as well as caves and tree holes, and in summer often in attics and lofts. They sometimes roost singly but more often in colonies, which are sometimes large, and usually hang free from the roof but also hang against walls or even in crevices; they may migrate over distances of up to 200km between summer and winter roosts. The Large Mouse-eared Bat is one of Europe's largest bats with a body length of up to 80mm and a wingspan of up to 45cm; it has fairly large ears, which, unlike those of Long-eared bats (p. 46), do not meet on top of the head. During the breeding season the females often form large nursery colonies in the warmest parts of their roost; the single young, which has greyer fur than an adult, starts to fly when about 45 days old.

The **Lesser Mouse-eared Bat** M. blythi is found mainly around the Mediterranean, including many of the islands, but also as far north as Hungary, Czechoslovakia and the southern USSR in the east; it is thought to occur in similar habitats to the Large Mouse-eared Bat and the 2 species are sometimes found in mixed colonies. The Lesser Mouse-eared is smaller than the Large – its body measures under 75mm – and has slightly narrower and more pointed ears but otherwise they are virtually identical. Mouse-eared bats are unlikely to be confused with any other species when seen at close quarters: they are larger than most other *Myotis* bats (pp. 30 and 34), lack a nose-leaf and the ears do not meet over the head.

MYOTIS BATS

Daubenton's Bat

Pond Bat

Daubenton's Bat *Myotis daubentoni* is widespread over most of Europe except in the south-east; it occurs in the British Isles and most of Scandinavia. It is fairly small (body length less than 50mm) and has large hind feet. Daubenton's Bats, often known as Water Bats, are usually found in well-wooded habitats near water where they may be seen skimming the surface as they hunt for insects; they may take insects and fish from the water. They roost in such places as hollow trees and buildings in summer and in caves and mines in winter, often hanging free but also in crevices.

The **Pond Bat** *M. dasycneme* is found in very similar habitats to Daubenton's Bat from eastern France and Switzerland eastwards through Germany. It is large, measuring up to 60mm in length, and generally hibernates from the roofs of caves; it apparently makes an audible scolding alarm call and is known to migrate frequently over long distances.

Geoffroy's Bat *M. emarginatus* has been recorded mainly in central and southern Europe but relatively little is known about it. It is small, with a body length of up to 50mm, and rather reddish. These 3 species may be confused with other *Myotis* bats, particularly the Whiskered bats (p. 30).

Geoffroy's Bat

BECHSTEIN'S BAT
Myotis bechsteini

Bechstein's Bat is found patchily from northern Spain westwards through Italy and France to the western USSR and northwards to southern England (where it is very rare) and Sweden. It is about the same size as the Common Long-eared Bat (50mm), but the ears, although long (up to 20mm), are smaller, broader and do not meet at the base. The fur is brownish above, paler below. They live in mainly wooded country and usually roost singly or in small colonies in tree holes (and nest boxes); in winter they hibernate in mines, caves and hollow trees; they normally hang from the roof or against the wall, rarely going in crevices. In summer the females form small nursery colonies. Bechstein's Bat may be confused with Long-eared bats (p. 46; see above), Barbastelle (opposite), or Mouse-eared bats (p. 32).

BARBASTELLE *Barbastella barbastellus*

The Barbastelle is found over most of Europe as far north as England and southern Scandinavia and is present on several Mediterranean islands; it is absent from most of the Balkans, much of southern Italy and much of Iberia. In the southern parts of its range it tends to live at higher altitudes. Barbastelles are found in a wide variety of habitats, ranging from open country to villages; in mountainous regions they are mainly found in forests. It is a medium-sized bat, with a body length of over 50mm. The ears are large and meet over the head, and the face has a characteristic wrinkled appearance; the ears and face are dark and the fur of the upperparts is dark brown, almost black, and is only slightly paler below. Barbastelles normally roost in crevices, behind bark on trees, and in other small cavities; more rarely they hang from the walls of caves in large groups, overlapping each other like shingles. They emerge fairly early in the evening and fly moderately high and fast. They may be confused with Long-eared bats (p. 46).

PIPISTRELLES

Savi's

Common

The 4 species of Pipistrelles are Europe's smallest bats. The **Common Pipistrelle** *Pipistrellus pipistrellus* is the most widespread being found almost everywhere except the extreme north and parts of Iberia; it is also often the most abundant in a wide variety of habitats including the centre of most towns and cities. It is the smallest species – the body can be as little as 33mm long with a wingspan of just over 20cm – and has rather short rounded ears and dark brown fur with a slightly paler belly. The Common Pipistrelle roosts throughout the year in tree holes, bird boxes, under eaves and tiles and in crevices, often in dense colonies; it is only rarely found in caves and then usually near the entrance. It occasionally flies in the day but usually emerges soon after dusk, often flying along a regular route with a characteristic twisting fluttering flight.

The 3 other species of Pipistrelle probably have similar habits to the Common Pipistrelle. **Savi's Pipistrelle** *P. savii* is mainly found in the Mediterranean in south-west France, Spain, Portugal, Italy, Yugoslavia, Greece and many of the islands including the Balearics, Corsica, Sardinia and Sicily. It has rounded ears and lighter coloured belly fur. **Kuhl's Pipistrelle** *P. kuhli* has a similar distribution to Savi's but is more widespread in western Iberia and France and is also found on Crete. **Nathusius' Pipistrelle** *P. nathusii* is found mostly in eastern Europe with only isolated populations in the west; it has been recorded in England. It has larger, broader ears than the Common Pipistrelle but is generally very similar in appearance and habits.

Kuhl's

NOCTULES

Common Noctule

The **Common Noctule** *Nyctalus noctula* is widespread and often locally abundant; it is found over most of Europe except northern Scandinavia, northern Scotland and Ireland; it is also found on many Mediterranean islands. Its typical habitat is open woodland and parklands. The Noctule is a large bat, with a body length of up to 80mm, a wingspan of up to 38cm and a weight of up to 40gm. The fur is a characteristic rich reddish brown; the ears are short and rounded with a very small tragus, and the muzzle is noticeably broad. Noctules normally roost in holes in trees both in summer and winter where they can often be located by the noise; occasionally they roost in buildings, but only exceptionally in caves. They emerge early in the evening, and fly high and fast, with sudden twisting dives. The voice in flight is often audible.

The **Lesser Noctule** or Leisler's Bat *N. leisleri* has a rather patchy distribution, particularly in western Europe, and is absent from much of the Mediterranean area and northern Europe; it is present in southern Britain and Ireland. In general appearance it is like a small, rather dark Common Noctule, growing to a body length of just over 60mm and weighing up to 20gm. Its habits are also similar but it sometimes roosts in buildings and also occurs more commonly in caves; it does not fly as high, nor dive so steeply. The **Greater Noctule** *N. lasiopterus* has been recorded from a number of localities in western Europe, from Spain, France and Switzerland eastwards to the Urals. It is larger than the Common Noctule (over 100mm) but very little else is known about it. Noctules are most likely to be confused with Serotines (p. 42).

Lesser Noctule

SEROTINES

The **Serotine** *Eptesicus serotinus* is widespread and often locally abundant in most parts of Europe as far north as southern England and Wales, Denmark and the Baltic coasts of Germany and Poland; it also occurs on many Mediterranean islands. It is found in a wide variety of habitats, particularly woodlands and parklands. The Serotine is a large, fairly heavily-built bat with a body length of up to 80mm, a wingspan of up to 38cm and a weight of up to 350gm. The ears are rounded, the tragus short; the fur is dark brown and the muzzle and ears are very dark. Serotines are often found near human habitation and frequently roost in hollow trees and rock crevices; in summer they are usually found in lofts, in winter in cellars and cracks in masonry but rarely in caves. They usually roost in colonies but may also be solitary. This species usually emerges early and flies fairly high; they have rather broad wings (compared with the narrower wings of the similar-sized Common Noctule, p. 40) and the flight is rather fluttering and lacks the sudden twisting dives of the Noctule, though the Serotine may occasionally swoop.

The **Northern Bat** *Eptesicus nilssoni* has a more restricted range than the Serotine and, as its name suggests, it occurs widely in Scandinavia and is the only bat north of the Arctic Circle; it extends southwards through Poland and the USSR to northern Romania and Hungary and occurs locally in Germany, France and Switzerland. In the southern parts of its range it is confined to mountainous regions, often above 200m, but is found in a wide variety of habitats further north. The Northern Bat grows up to 55mm long and in general appearance is rather like a small Serotine with longer, less rounded ears and yellowish-tinged upperparts. In summer, they frequently roost in buildings, tree holes, rock crevices or under bark; in winter, in cellars, cracks in masonry and also in buildings. They emerge from their roost fairly early. They are most likely to be confused with the Serotine or the Noctules (p. 40).

Northern Bat

43

BATS

Schreiber's

Parti-coloured

Schreiber's Bat *Miniopterus schreibersi* is found in the Mediterranean region and eastwards through Romania to the south-western USSR. It is a medium-sized bat, generally similar to the Noctules (p. 40) and Pipistrelles (p. 38) but intermediate in size; the strongly domed head is characteristic. They are rarely found near human habitation but often in caves, mines and deserted buildings; they are often found in mixed colonies with *Myotis* bats.

The **Parti-coloured Bat** *Vespertilio murinus* is found in central and eastern Europe as far north as southern Scandinavia and as far south as northern Greece. It is a fairly large bat, only slightly smaller than the Common Noctule (p. 40) and the Serotine

(p. 42), and is distinctively bicoloured – almost white on the underside with brown white-tipped hairs on the upperparts. It roosts in hollow trees, rock clefts and buildings; it has been recorded as a vagrant in Britain.

The **European Free-tailed Bat** *Tadarida teniotis* is confined to the Mediterranean zone including most of the islands where it is locally abundant. It is the largest European bat, with a body length of up to 87mm, is very heavily built and has distinctive ears and a wrinkled face which gives it the alternative name of Mastiff Bat. Its long (up to 57mm) fleshy tail is free of membrane for over one third of its total length. This species is often found in buildings and even in towns; it emits an audible ringing sound in flight and a rattling noise as it leaves its roost. The **Egyptian Hollow-faced Bat** *Nycteris thebaica* has only once been recorded in Europe, on Corfu.

**European
Free-tailed**

LONG-EARED BATS

Grey Long-eared

Common
Long-eared

The **Common Long-eared Bat** *Plecotus auritus* is very widespread and inhabits most parts of Europe, except northern Scandinavia, and most islands, though it is less abundant in the south; it is found mainly in well-wooded areas, as well as parks, gardens and often in towns and villages. The Common Long-eared Bat is a medium-sized bat, with a body length of up to about 50mm, and enormous ears nearly as long as the body; when at rest the ears are folded under the wings, with the long, slender tragus projecting. They roost in buildings and trees, but rarely in caves, and then normally at the entrance. They often roost singly, but the females gather in clusters during the breeding season. Long-eared bats often fly among trees, hovering and picking insects and spiders off leaves.

The **Grey Long-eared Bat** *P. austriacus* is very closely related to the Common Long-eared Bat, and its distribution is still not fully known. It has been recorded from France, eastwards to Poland and Czechoslovakia, and it is also known in England. In appearance the Grey Long-eared Bat is very similar to the Common Long-eared Bat; as its name suggests, it is slightly greyer, but otherwise only distinguished with certainty by measurements. As far as is known it is also similar to the Common Long-eared Bat in its habits. Long-eared bats are most likely to be confused with the Barbastelle (p. 37) which has much shorter, though large, dark ears which meet over the head; and Bechstein's Bat (p. 36) which has smaller, more pointed ears.

HORSESHOE BATS

**Lesser
Horseshoe Bat**

The **Lesser Horseshoe Bat** *Rhinolophus hipposideros* is the most widespread of the Horseshoe bats in Europe, ranging over the entire western and Mediterranean parts of Europe as far north as southwestern Ireland and southern Britain, the Netherlands and northern Germany, Poland and east through the southern USSR. The **Mediterranean Horseshoe Bat** *R. euryale* is found mainly in the Mediterranean zones of Europe; **Blasius' Horse-**

shoe Bat *R. blasii* is a little known species found in Italy, Sicily and south-eastern Europe; and **Mehely's Horseshoe Bat** *R. mehelyi* is also a predominantly Mediterranean species but its distribution is very poorly known. The main differences between these bats are in the shape of the nose-leaf and in size: the Lesser grows to just over 60mm and weighs less than 10gm; Blasius' is slightly larger, the Mediterranean larger still and Mehely's nearly as large as the Greater Horseshoe (p. 50). Like the Greater Horseshoe, these species are found in well-wooded country, roost hanging free and may hang in clusters or singly. At close quarters Horseshoe bats are not likely to be confused with other European bats, but outside northern Europe positive identification is very difficult.

Lesser
Horseshoes
at roost

Mediterranean

Blasius'

Mehely's

49

GREATER HORSESHOE BAT
Rhinolophus ferrumequinum

The Greater Horseshoe Bat is found throughout most of Europe as far north as southern Britain and the Netherlands, northern Germany and eastwards to southern Poland and the USSR; it is found on most Mediterranean islands. However, it has declined in many areas and in Britain is now on the verge of extinction. It is found mainly in wooded country, roosting in caves, tree holes, cellars and mines in winter, and in attics, lofts, cellars and outbuildings in summer. It grows to a length of nearly 70mm, has a wingspan of up to 38cm and a weight of up to 28gm. It is the largest of the Horseshoe bats, which are characterised by their distinctive nose-leaf – an outgrowth of naked skin used in the production of pulses of ultra-sonic sound for echo location. The Greater Horseshoe Bat emerges rather late and its flight is rather low and flapping with frequent glides. It roosts both solitarily and in large clusters and like other Horseshoe bats it always sleeps suspended from the roof with the wings wrapped around the body. It can be distinguished from other species of Horseshoe bat (p. 48) by its larger size.

adult in flight

at roost

BROWN HARE
Lepus capensis

×⅓

fore

hind

The Brown Hare is widespread throughout Europe except northern Scandinavia, the Alps and the higher altitudes in Britain and Scandinavia. It is found on all the larger Mediterranean islands and on many smaller ones; it has been introduced into Ireland and the Orkneys. Brown Hares occur in practically all habitats, but prefer cultivated lands and open deciduous woodlands. Comparatively large, it grows to a weight of 6kg (but usually less) and a length of up to 70cm and is characterised by long black-tipped ears and black on top of the rather short tail; the Mediterranean Brown Hare is small with mottled back and white feet. Although hares are mainly active by night, they are frequently seen by day; they are very swift, running with a powerful leaping gait. They do not make a nest or burrow, but merely scrape a 'form' in the soil; the 2–4 young (leverets) are born fully furred, can run within a day and are weaned a week later. Hares often congregate, particularly in spring, when the males fight and pursue the females (giving rise to the expression 'mad as a March hare'). Hares feed on grasses, herbs, roots, crops and the bark and shoots of trees. Brown Hares are most likely to be confused with Varying Hares (p. 54) which are smaller and greyish or white, or Rabbits (p. 56) which are smaller, greyer and have shorter ears.

VARYING HARE *Lepus timidus*

adult male,
summer
pelage

The Varying Hare (also known as the Arctic, Mountain or Blue Hare) occurs throughout the tundra and taiga zones of the northern hemisphere. In Europe it is found in Scandinavia, Finland and the eastern USSR, and as isolated populations in Iceland, Scotland, the Faeroes, Ireland and the Alps; it has been introduced into England and Wales. At lower latitudes it is a mountain species living at higher altitudes than the Brown Hare. There is considerable geographical variation, but the Varying Hare grows

hind, snow

to a maximum length of about 60cm and a weight of up to 5.8kg; the ears are up to 9.5cm, and would just reach the muzzle-tip if laid forward. Except in Ireland, the Faeroes and the lower altitudes in Scotland and Scandinavia, these hares turn pure white in winter apart from black ear-tips. Populations which do not turn white, and animals in summer pelage, are distinguished from Brown Hares (p. 52), by their smaller size, proportionally shorter ears, and often greyer coloration. Varying Hares are often gregarious particularly in winter, and are frequently seen in daylight. They make their nests (forms) in rock clefts, occasionally excavating a short tunnel. They scream when injured, and utter a whistle as an alarm call. Breeding starts in late winter or early spring; there are usually 2 or 3 young (leverets) per litter and up to 3 litters a year. Varying Hares are important prey species for a number of birds and mammals. They may be confused with Brown Hares but their ranges do not often overlap.

winter pelage

55

RABBIT *Oryctolagus cuniculus*

adults

young
18 days

$\times \frac{1}{3}$

fore

hind

Originally from north-west Africa and Iberia, the Rabbit has been introduced and spread to much of Europe and many other parts of the world. In Europe Rabbits are found as far east as Poland, Hungary and the USSR; they are also found on the Balearics, Sicily, Sardinia and Corsica, in most of the British Isles and parts of Scandinavia. They occupy virtually any habitat that provides grass and herbage for grazing, and sufficient soil for them to excavate burrows. Rabbits grow to about 45cm, have a short (less than 80mm) tail, and weigh up to about 2.2kg. The most distinctive features are the short, white, fluffy tail, and long ears (up to 70mm) though proportionally shorter than those of hares. Rabbits are usually brown but black individuals or other colour variants occur. Rabbits are mainly active at dawn and dusk; they live colonially in warrens, but occasionally live entirely above ground. Four to six young make up a normal litter size and they are mature at about 3 months. They feed mainly on grass and herbage, in hard weather rabbits will gnaw bark, and even climb trees. Their droppings are often deposited in regular latrines on mole- or anthills. Rabbits are most likely to be confused with Brown Hares (p. 52) or, in summer, with Varying Hares (p. 54). Cottontail Rabbits, *Sylvilagus*, from America, have been introduced into Italy and France.

SQUIRRELS

Continental Red Squirrel

winter

summer

British Red Squirrels

The **Red Squirrel** *Sciurus vulgaris* is widespread in Europe, and often common, even in towns. It has been displaced by the Grey Squirrel (p. 60) in much of England and Wales and is absent from most Mediterranean islands. It is found in a variety of woodland and forest habitats, with a preference for coniferous woodlands. Red Squirrels grow to a total length of over 30cm, of which the bushy

eaten pine cone

tail is less than half, and are usually reddish brown; in summer, British squirrels have an almost white tail. They build several untidy nests (dreys) of twigs and branches, sometimes in hollow trees, and in winter may spend most or all of the day inside. There are 2 litters a year of 3–7 young which become independent at about 2 months old and mature at 1 year. They feed on a wide variety of shoots, nuts, berries, fungi, insects and the eggs and young of birds.

The **Flying Squirrel** *Pteromys volans* is found in the coniferous and birch forests of north-western Europe as far west as Finland and Poland. It is much smaller than the Red Squirrel – more dormouse sized – growing up to 17cm with a tail of up to 13cm; it is very secretive and emerges only at dusk; during the winter it hibernates. Despite its name, it does not fly but glides on the membrane which stretches between the fore- and hind-legs. An Asiatic species, the **Persian Squirrel** *S. anomalus*, is found on the Greek island of Lesbos.

**Flying
Squirrel**

GREY SQUIRREL *Sciurus carolinensis*

winter pelage

summer pelage

$\times \frac{1}{2}$

fore

hind

Originally a native of the deciduous woodlands of eastern North America, the Grey Squirrel was introduced into Britain and Ireland, and is now widespread and abundant. It has largely displaced the native Red Squirrel which is, in many regions, confined to more extensive tracts of coniferous forests, and is totally extinct in most of lowland Britain. The Grey Squirrel is slightly larger than the Red, and grows to a length of up to 30cm, plus a tail of up to 25cm, and a weight of up to 750gm. Although normally grey, the back can often be reddish brown, and there is always a brownish colour on the flanks; however, the Grey Squirrel always lacks ear tufts – which the Red Squirrel has in winter. The Grey Squirrel is diurnal, and spends more time on the ground than the Red. It builds its nest (drey) in holes in trees, in the lofts of buildings, or in the fork of a tree, close to the trunk. It makes a variety of chattering noises; its feeding habits are similar to the Red Squirrel's. It can be distinguished from the Red Squirrel (p. 58) by range and coloration.

drey

MARMOTS

The 2 species of marmot found in Europe are the
Alpine Marmot *Marmota marmota* and the **Bobak
Marmot** *M. bobak*, also known as the Steppe Marmot. The first is usually found in alpine pastures
above the treeline (though it can range from
1,300–3,000m) in the Alps, the Carpathians and in
the Pyrenees where it has been introduced; the
second is restricted to the steppes of the southern
USSR. Both species are very similar in appearance
and habits, though the Bobak Marmot has rather
more uniformly coloured fur and a shorter tail, and

Alpine Marmot

they will be described together. Marmots are rather thickset animals growing to around 70cm with a short tail of around 15cm and weighing up to 8kg; they are active by day and feed on plant material. They live in colonies which excavate extensive burrows usually with entrances on south-facing slopes. Marmots characteristically sit on their haunches to watch for predators and can emit loud warning whistles which will send a whole colony underground. During winter the colony hibernates; breeding takes place in spring and the females give birth to litters of 2–4 young. The 2 species cannot be confused as their ranges do not overlap.

Bobak Marmot

SOUSLIKS

Two species of souslik, or ground squirrel, are found in south-eastern Europe: the **Spotted Souslik** *Spermophilus suslicus* on the east European steppes from south-eastern Poland and north-eastern Romania, eastwards through Russia, and the **European Souslik** *Spermophilus citellus* in open steppe country from south-eastern Germany and southern Poland, southwards to Bulgaria, eastern Yugoslavia and northern Greece. Both species inhabit open country, and are often seen along roads and killed by passing cars. The European Souslik measures 22cm with a tail of up to 75mm and weighs up to 340gm; the Spotted Souslik is a similar size but has a shorter tail (up to 40mm) and is spotted. Both species are active by day and make a wide variety of whistles and

European Souslik

growls; they often stand upright to keep watch for predators and when alarmed emit a short high-pitched whistle. Sousliks live in colonies and excavate burrows which are often deep and extensive, and usually have some vertical entrances. They can be serious pests as they feed mainly on grain and seeds which they gather in their cheek pouches and store in their tunnels. Hibernation takes place during winter and immediately after they start breeding, producing a single litter of 6–8 young about 1 month later. Sousliks are unlikely to be confused with other species within their range and habitats.

Spotted Souslik

BEAVERS

European Beaver

The **Beaver** *Castor fiber* was once found throughout most of Europe except the Mediterranean zones. Due to over-hunting (for fur and castoreum – from the scent glands) it has been reduced to a few isolated colonies on the Rhône (France), the Elbe (Germany), in southern Norway and European Russia. It is extinct in the rest of Europe, including Britain, but has been extensively reintroduced in many parts of Scandinavia, the USSR, Germany and Switzerland. The almost identical **American Beaver** *Castor canadensis* has been introduced into Finland and is now well-established. Both species prefer well-wooded, slow-flowing rivers and marshes with undergrowth.

The Beaver is the largest native European rodent, growing to a total length of up to 130cm, of which the tail is about one third, and weighing over 30kg. Scandinavian Beavers are smaller and darker in colour than those from the south of France. The most distinctive features of the Beavers are the heavily built body, large blunt-muzzled head, small ears, and the very large, spatulate tail covered with scales; the hind feet are webbed, the fore-feet strongly clawed for digging. Beavers are mainly nocturnal, feeding on bark, shoots, aquatic plants, thistles and other vegetation. Extensive 'lodges' are built (though only rarely by the Rhône Beavers); they also tunnel into banks and build dams and canals to regulate the water level. Beavers swim and dive well and can stay submerged for up to 15 minutes, but more usually for about 5; when diving in alarm they slap their tail

67

on the surface of the water as a signal. They pair for life, and have a single litter of 2–4 young each year; the young do not become fully independent until they are nearly 3 years old, and so a family group may have young of different ages in it. Beavers are shy and rarely seen, but the signs they leave behind them are distinctive: the gnawed stumps of small trees up to 20cm in diameter (particularly willow, aspen, ash, oak, birch, alder and poplar), dams and canals; and pats of mud on which scent is deposited. They do not hibernate in winter, but, particularly in the northern parts of their range, they spend much of the time in their lodges or burrows feeding on stores of twigs and bark. The only other animals with which Beavers are likely to be confused are Musk Rats (p. 82) or Coypu (p. 118) which lack the flattened tail and are smaller, or possibly Otters (p. 146) which are much more slender.

hind

fore

$\times \frac{1}{3}$

lodge

tail slapping
in alarm

69

HAMSTERS

The **Common Hamster** *Cricetus cricetus* is found from north-eastern France eastwards through Germany and south-east to Romania and Bulgaria; the **Romanian Hamster** *Mesocricetus newtoni* in a small area of Romania and Bulgaria; the **Grey Hamster** *C. migratorius* in the southern USSR, with a few isolated populations in Bulgaria and Greece. They all occur in open, dry country, often steppes, or agricultural land where they can be serious pests. The **Golden Hamster**

**Common
Hamster**

M. auratus is a popular pet, closely related to the Romanian Hamster, which has occasionally escaped and become established in the wild for short periods. The Common Hamster is a relatively large animal, growing to over 30cm long and weighing over 350gm; the Grey Hamster grows to less than half that size (up to 12cm and a weight of around 35gm); the Romanian Hamster is midway, measuring 15–18cm in length and weighing 80–150gm. All 3 have very short tails: that of the Romanian Hamster is almost invisible. The Common Hamster is unmistakable on account of its large size, black underparts and the pale patches on its sides; the Romanian Hamster has distinctive piebald markings on its neck and shoulders; the diminutive Grey Hamster can be distinguished from similar-sized voles (pp. 84–91) by larger eyes and ears and its pale greyish colour.

Romanian Hamster

Grey Hamster

VOLES AND LEMMINGS

Introduction

Voles and Lemmings are a distinctive group of blunt-headed, short-legged rodents, with small beady eyes, that are widely distributed and often abundant in Europe. They breed rapidly and some species, particularly in the north, may build up to plague proportions every 4 years or so. They are mainly vegetarian, though most species will eat molluscs and other invertebrates occasionally. In turn they are prey items for a number of animals and birds including foxes, Weasels, Stoats, martens, cats, eagles, buzzards, harriers, owls, some snakes and even lizards and toads. Most species are rather secretive, living in tunnels or runs hidden in vegetation. There are 21 species of voles and lemmings which fall into the following 8 groups:

Field voles *Microtus* (p. 88) are usually brownish, with small ears and short tails; they are difficult to differentiate from the Pine voles. The **Musk Rat** *Ondatra* (p. 82) is a large animal characterised by webbed hind feet. **Martino's Snow Vole** *Dinaromys* (p. 90) is found only in the Balkans; its tail is over half the body length. The **Norway Lemming** *Lemmus* (p. 74) is a boldly patterned lemming. **Pine voles** *Pitymys* (pp. 84–7) are difficult to differentiate from the Field voles as both are usually brownish, with small ears and short tails. **Redbacked voles** *Clethrionomys* (p. 78) are characterised by reddish fur on the back and fairly prominent ears. **Water voles** *Arvicola* (p. 80) are brown or blackish medium-sized voles over 15cm in length. The **Wood Lemming** *Myopus* (p. 77) has grey fur with a brown streak on the back.

NORWAY LEMMING   *Lemmus lemmus*

The Norway Lemming is found in the mountains and taiga and tundra of Norway and Sweden, eastwards through Finland and the USSR to the White Sea; in 'Lemming Years' (see below) it is more widespread. Its preferred habitat is the sub-alpine birch and willow zone up to near the snow line where there are a variety of dwarf trees and shrubs, mosses, sedges, grasses and berried plants. The Norway Lemming grows to about 16cm, including a short tail of less than 20mm, and weighs up to 45gm. The fur is distinctively patterned, but the proportions of black and yellow vary considerably. Lemmings burrow extensively in summer, and in winter they make tunnels beneath the snow, or the surface of the ground. Normally they have 2 litters of between 4–8 young, which are born in summer; occasionally the breeding season is extended, and they have even bred beneath snow; the young can breed when about 5 weeks old. Norway Lemmings feed almost exclusively on plants; they are, in turn, important prey for a wide variety of mammals and birds. The Norway Lemming is famous for its population explosions; there is a regular cycle, of approximately 4 years, when population density reaches a peak, food supplies become exhausted and occasionally massive emigrations take place, when they stream down the mountains, even swimming rivers and crossing lakes that block their passage. If the water is rough vast numbers may drown – and this has probably given rise to the myth that lemmings commit mass suicide. Norway Lemmings are not likely to be confused with any other species occurring in their habitat; all other voles and lemmings lack the parti-coloured pattern.

tunnels

ARCTIC LEMMING *Dicrostonyx torquatus*

summer

winter

The Arctic or Varying Lemming is found in arctic tundra from the shores of the White Sea eastwards, through Siberia. It grows to a little over 11cm and weighs just over 57gm. In the summer it is brownish with a distinctive pale collar, and a well-defined reddish spot above each ear; in winter it is one of the few rodents to turn white. Arctic Lemmings are active by day (during the arctic summer) and build their nest in rock clefts, in burrows, or (in winter) on the ground surface, beneath snow. Although populations fluctuate, they do not show the same dramatic trends as the Norway Lemming (p. 74). In summer this species may be confused with voles (p. 78) and other lemmings.

WOOD LEMMING   *Myopus schisticolor*

The Wood Lemming is found in Norway, Sweden, Finland, Russia and eastwards through Siberia, mainly in coniferous forests but also in tundra and wet mossy habitats. It grows to about 95mm, with a short tail of less than 20mm, and weighs up to 30gm. The fur colour is mainly dark grey (even on the underside) with a characteristic rufous patch on the back; in winter the colouring is paler. Wood Lemmings burrow among mosses and roots, and they are apparently the only small mammal in Europe to feed mainly on mosses, lichens and liverworts. They breed from June to August, and 2 litters of up to 7 young are produced. Population numbers fluctuate and although mass emigrations do occur, they are less frequent and on a smaller scale than those of the Norway Lemming (p. 74). The Wood Lemming may be confused with the Red-backed voles (p. 78), which have longer tails and are not nearly as grey.

RED-BACKED VOLES

Bank Vole

The 3 Red-backed voles described on these 2 pages are members of a group found throughout the northern latitudes of the northern hemisphere. The **Bank Vole** *Clethrionomys glareolus* is the more widespread of the 3, being found in a variety of usually well-wooded habitats, hedgerows and even gardens over most of Europe. The **Ruddy Vole** *C. rutilus* is restricted to the tundra, pine and birch zones of the Arctic; the **Grey-sided Vole** *C. rufocanus* ranges a little further south but is confined to Scandinavia and the USSR. In winter the Ruddy and Bank Voles often enter houses and farm buildings. All 3 species measure 80–130mm in length but the Grey-sided is generally the largest of the 3; in addition both Grey-sided and Ruddy Voles have tails of under 40mm, while the Bank Vole's is usually over 40mm. All 3 feed on fruits, seeds, nuts, roots, stems and some insects; the Grey-sided eats coarser vegetation associated with its habitat. Four or more litters of around 6 young are produced per season. In the north of their range numbers fluctuate enormously; they are also extensively preyed on by a wide variety of birds, animals and reptiles and are frequently found in owl pellets. They are most likely to be confused with other voles (pp. 84–91) but are generally redder and have more prominent ears than the other species within their range.

× 1⅓

fore

hind

Ruddy Vole

Grey-sided Vole

WATER VOLES

Water voles are found in a wide variety of habitats, often far from water; the **Water Vole** *Arvicola terrestris* in northern Iberia, Britain and eastern France, eastwards through most of central and northern Europe, the **Western Water Vole** or **Ground Vole** *A. sapidus* in France and Iberia. Both species are

80

extremely similar and also rather variable so that it is often extraordinarily difficult to distinguish between them. Both grow to a length of about 30cm of which the tail is less than half, and weigh up to 280gm; where the 2 occur together, the Water Vole is the larger. Water voles tunnel extensively in banks and also on the surface of the ground; they are active by day, make extensive runs along the edges of river banks and leave small heaps of droppings in prominent places. The 3–6 young are born in a nest of roots and grasses. Water voles feed mainly on reeds, grasses, sedges, rhizomes and other vegetation, including crops and also small amounts of animal food. They are most likely to be confused with other voles (pp. 78, 84–91) all of which are smaller, or the Brown Rat (p. 104) which is larger, and has a more pointed muzzle and a large tapering tail.

Ground Vole

MUSK RAT *Ondatra zibethicus*

Musk Rat

Originally from North America, the Musk Rat is a fur-bearer which has been introduced into many parts of Europe; it colonised parts of Britain in the 1920s but was exterminated in 1937. It is the largest species of vole, growing to a length of 24–34cm, with a tail of up to 26cm, and weighing 800–1,600gm. The fur is a rich brown, the belly silvery. The long, naked, scaly, black, compressed tail is extremely distinctive and the best guide to identification. The fore-feet are not webbed, the hind feet are. Musk Rats are found in lakes

droppings

fore

hind

and slow-flowing rivers with dense cover on the banks where they often excavate complex tunnel systems. In marshes they build conical lodges of twigs, up to 1m high. They feed on most species of aquatic and riverside plants, and also some animal matter, such as molluscs; in some areas they are also serious pests of crops, particularly root crops. Musk Rats are active by day as well as night, and they mark their territories with the musk from which they take their name. Like the closely related voles they produce several litters a season of between 4 and 8 young. Musk Rats are only likely to be confused with Beavers (p. 66) or Coypu (p. 118) – but are easily identified by their distinctive tail and smaller size. Young ones might be confused with Water voles (p. 80), which have short tails.

Beaver

Coypu

Musk Rat

83

PINE VOLES

European Pine Vole

Alpine Pine Vole

The Pine voles (*Pitymys* species) are a widely distributed, closely related group superficially very similar to the Field voles (p. 88) and the Red-backed voles (p. 78); one or more species of Pine vole is found over most of central and southern Europe, but they are absent from most islands. They are generally up to about 100mm long with, in addition, a rather short tail of usually less than 30mm; their ears are shorter than most other voles' (notably Red-backed voles) and the fur colour is often more reddish or darker than the Field Voles. However, as is often the case with burrowing rodents, they are virtually impossible to identify with any certainty in the field. Pine voles live in a wide variety of habitats, but typically in open woodlands, cultivated lands, meadows and steppes; despite their common name, they are not particularly abundant in coniferous woods. They all spend most of their lives underground occasionally making small humps of earth, usually smaller and less obvious than those of moles (p. 26) or *Arvicola* voles (p. 80). They feed mainly on roots, grasses and other vegetation; the breeding season is probably longer than most other voles'. Although little is known of their habits, most Pine voles are probably active by day but keep underground.

The **Alpine Pine Vole** *P. multiplex*, also known as Fatio's Pine Vole, is confined to the southern side of the Alps in France, Italy, Switzerland and Austria; it is found mainly in the alpine meadows.

The **Balkan Pine Vole** *P. thomasia* is found from south-western Yugoslavia to Greece.

The **Bavarian Pine Vole** *P. bavaricus* is found only in the alpine meadows of a small area in Bavaria

habitat of
Alpine Pine Vole

Savi's Pine Vole

Mediterranean Pine Vole

and is distinguished by its very small ears. Possibly extinct.

The **Dalmatian Pine Vole** *P. liechtensteini* is confined to north-western Yugoslavia.

The **European Pine Vole** *P. subterraneus* is the most widespread and best known of the Pine voles; it is found from France eastwards through central Europe to Russia usually in woodlands or open country including steppes and farmlands. They are known to produce up to 9 litters a year, but normally with only 2 or 3 young per litter. They excavate extensive tunnel systems close to the ground surface. European Pine voles are often very numerous but where Field voles are common they are often rare or absent and *vice versa*.

The **Lusitanian Pine Vole** *P. lusitanicus* is found in north-western Iberia and south-western France.

The **Mediterranean Pine Vole** *P. duodecimcostatus* is one of the most widespread species of Pine voles and is found from south-eastern France through eastern and southern Spain.

The **Tatra Pine Vole** *P. tatricus* is a rather large species found only above the treeline in the alpine meadows of the Tatra Mountains.

Savi's Pine Vole *P. savii* lives in the mountains of south-western France, north-western Spain and Italy; it may also occur in Macedonia but this may be a distinct species.

habitat of
Bavarian Pine Vole

FIELD VOLES

Common Vole

Field Vole

The **Common Vole** (*Microtus arvalis*) is widespread and often abundant in mainland Europe from France eastwards to the USSR and south-eastern Europe; it is not found in Greece, in most of Italy or Scandinavia, and there are only isolated populations in Spain; isolated populations occur in the Orkneys. The **Field** or **Short-tailed Vole** (*M. agrestis*) is found from northern Portugal eastwards through central and eastern Europe and north through Britain to the Arctic Circle; it is absent from much of southern Europe and Ireland. The **Northern** or **Root Vole** (*M. oeconomus*) is widespread in the taiga and tundra zones of northern Europe and extends as far south as northern Germany; there are scattered populations in the Netherlands, Germany, Poland, Czechoslovakia and Hungary. Another species *M. epiroticus* is only distinguishable from the Common Vole by differences in chromosomes; it is only found in eastern Europe. These 4 species of vole are similar in appearance and habits. The Northern Vole is the darkest and grows to a length of 150mm with a tail of nearly 65mm. The Common and Field Voles are smaller, usually 95–130mm plus a tail of 25–45mm; at close range the Field Vole can be seen to have hairy ears whereas the Common Vole's are naked. These voles live among coarse grasses and dense vegetation and in tunnels; they feed on vegetable matter, but may eat insects and small animals. They are probably the most important mammalian prey species in Europe. They may be confused with various other species of vole.

Northern Vole

VOLES

Martino's Snow Vole

Snow Vole

Martino's Snow Vole *Dinaromys bogdanovi* (also known as **Nehring's Snow Vole** *Dolomys milleri*) is found only in the mountains of western Yugoslavia and Albania where it inhabits rocky areas between 600–2,000m in the grass and woodland zones. It is a rather large species and grows to a length of nearly 15cm with an exceptionally long tail of nearly 12cm; it has dense grey Chinchilla-like fur.

The **Snow Vole** *Microtus nivalis* occurs in isolated populations in many of the mountain ranges of central and southern Europe, from Spain in the west to the Tatras and Carpathians in the east; it is found mainly above the treeline in alpine meadows but lower in France. In general appearance it is similar to the closely related Northern Vole (p. 89); it is large, growing to a body length of up to 14cm, with a very characteristic whitish tail of up to 75mm, and has long soft light-grey fur. Like most voles it tunnels, often among rocks, but it is not particularly secretive and often emerges to sun itself. It apparently dries leaves and grass and then stores them with nuts, seeds, and berries inside the tunnel.

The **Social Vole** *M. guentheri* is found in southern Russia and south-eastern Europe. It is very closely related (and very similar in appearance) to the **Iberian Vole** *M. cabrerae*; it is also similar in appearance to the Common Vole (p. 88) and grows to about 12.5cm plus a short tail of up to 40mm. It burrows extensively and is often found in open country, including arable land. Social Voles occasionally build up to plague densities.

Social Vole

MOLE-RATS

**Lesser
Mole-rat**

Greater Mole-rat

The 2 species of mole-rat found in Europe are the **Greater Mole-rat** *Spalax micropthalmus* and the **Lesser Mole-rat** *S. leucodon*. Both species inhabit open steppes, woodlands and cultivated lands: the Lesser Mole-rat in Greece, Yugoslavia and Bulgaria, north to Hungary and southern Russia; the Greater Mole-rat in eastern Romania, southern

Russia and a few places in Bulgaria and Greece. The Lesser Mole-rat grows to around 25cm and a weight of 220gm; the Greater Mole-rat to about 30cm and 500gm. Both species are adapted for a subterranean life: the tail is virtually absent, the eyes covered by skin and there are no external ears; the fur is dense and soft, except along the side of the head which has a row of stiff bristles; the head is flattened to bulldoze soft soil and the incisors enlarged for digging. Extensive tunnel systems are built with chambers for nests, food stores and latrines and larger mounds of earth are thrown up than by moles. Mole-rats feed on roots, tubers, bulbs and other underground parts of plants. Mainly nocturnal, mole-rats occasionally emerge to sun themselves. They are not likely to be confused with any other species.

RATS AND MICE

Introduction

Rats and mice are a widely distributed group of rodents in Europe, which are rather variable in size and appearance. The muzzle is characteristically more pointed than that of voles, but less pointed than that of shrews, and the upper lip is divided. Several species are found in Europe as a direct result of man's activities and several are found close to man's habitations. Most rats and mice are important prey items for a variety of mammal and bird predators, and also reptiles. The main groups of rats and mice are:

The **Harvest Mouse** *Micromys* species (p. 96) which is a tiny reddish brown mouse with a prehensile tail and small eyes.

The **House Mouse** *Mus* species (p. 106), which is usually greyish and commonly associated with man and arable land.

Rats *Rattus* species (pp. 102–5) which are large usually brown, greyish or blackish and usually associated with man's habitation.

Wood mice *Apodemus* species (p. 98) which are usually yellowish brown or reddish brown, with long tails, large eyes and ears.

The relative abundance of different rats and mice in an area can be discovered by analysing the pellets of birds of prey which contain the fur and bones of small mammals. By soaking these pellets in water the prey items can be identified from the bones, particularly by the skulls they contain. A number of identification guides to the bones are available and are listed in the bibliography on p. 6.

Brown Rat

Wood Mouse

House Mouse

Harvest Mouse

HARVEST MOUSE
Micromys minutus

The Harvest Mouse is widely distributed in Europe and is found from north-west Spain, north to southern Britain, Denmark and southern Finland, and eastward to the USSR, Greece and Bulgaria, but it is absent from the higher altitudes and from most of the Mediterranean areas. It is primarily an animal of a rather specialised habitat, the 'stalk zone', living among the stems of reeds, cereal crops, hedgerows and weeds on waste ground. The Harvest Mouse is the smallest European rodent, with a body of up to about 75mm and a slightly shorter tail; it weighs 5–9gm. The most distinctive features, apart from its size, are its partly prehensile tail and rather reddish upperparts with a white underside. Active by day and night, it climbs among stems and branches with agility, using its tail as support. They build nests about the size of a cricket ball, of loosely woven grasses, around the stems of grasses, reeds or corn; these are most obvious in winter when the herbage has died back. Several litters are born each year, of up to 6 young. Harvest Mice feed principally on seeds, berries, shoots, buds and insects. A new species of very large Harvest Mouse with a long tail was recently described in Romania, but it is probably only a local variant. Harvest Mice are most likely to be confused with Birch Mice (p. 114), Wood mice (p. 98), or House Mice (p. 106).

nest

WOOD MICE

Wood Mouse

The **Wood Mouse** *Apodemus sylvaticus* is often abundant in most parts of Europe except northern Scandinavia and Finland; it is found on many islands including Iceland, Ireland, the Faeroes and many smaller islands around north-west Europe. It occurs in a wide variety of habitats, but where the Yellow-necked Mouse also occurs it tends to be found in more open country. The Wood Mouse grows to a total length of about 20cm of which the tail is just over half, and weighs up to 25gm. Wood mice are omnivores, mainly nocturnal and extremely agile; they also tunnel extensively. They breed throughout the warmer months producing several litters a year of up to 9 young (usually 4–6).

The **Yellow-necked Mouse** *A. flavicollis* is found mainly in eastern and central Europe, north to Scandinavia and Finland and west to eastern and southern France, and in southern England and Wales. It is similar to the closely related Wood Mouse and where the 2 occur together it is more characteristic of mature woodland. It is larger than the Wood Mouse, growing to a total length of about 22cm of which the tail is over half, and, although very similar in appearance, it always has a yellowish brown bar or patch on the throat. These 2 Wood mice are most likely to be confused with other Wood mice, the House Mouse (p. 106), and the Harvest Mouse (p. 96).

Yellow-necked Mouse

WOOD MICE

**Rock
Mouse**

The **Rock Mouse** *Apodemus mystacinus* is found in
dry rocky habitats in south-eastern Europe from the
Dalmatian coast of Yugoslavia southwards to
Bulgaria, Albania, Greece and Turkey; it also occurs
on Rhodes. It is the largest of the Wood mice,
growing to 15cm with a tail of nearly the same length;
otherwise it is very similar to the other species although the upperparts are greyer. It is most likely to
be confused with other Wood mice, all of which are
smaller.

The **Striped Field Mouse** *A. agrarius* is found in
woodlands, hedgerows and farmlands mainly in eastern Europe from northern Germany and Italy eastwards through Poland, Czechoslovakia, Hungary,

Romania and the USSR; it also occurs in Macedonia. It is slightly smaller than the Wood Mouse (p. 98), growing to a total length of about 17cm of which the tail is less than half, but is best distinguished by the black stripe down the middle of the back; in winter the fur is greyer. Like other Wood mice it feeds on a wide variety of vegetable and animal matter but it is less nocturnal. It is most likely to be confused with Birch mice (p. 114) which have longer prehensile tails.

The other European species of Wood mouse is the **Eastern Wood Mouse** *A. microps*, also known as the Lesser Wood Mouse, which occurs in eastern Europe; both species are very similar to the Wood Mouse (p. 98) but the former is paler and greyer, the latter found in more open country.

**Striped
Field
Mouse**

BLACK RAT *Rattus rattus*

anti-rat
baffle

brown
phase

black
phase

× 1

fore

hind

young

Originally from southern Asia, the Black Rat (also known as the Ship or House Rat) now has a worldwide distribution; in Europe it has largely been displaced by the Brown Rat particularly in Britain and Scandinavia. Total length is about 45cm of which the tail is just over half, and it weighs 150–200gm. The colouring is variable, but often blackish above and smoky below. They are opportunistic feeders, mainly nocturnal and very sociable. They breed throughout the year, with up to 5 litters a year of 5–10 young, which mature in less than 4 months. It is most likely to be confused with the Brown Rat (p. 104) but the Black Rat has a more pointed muzzle, and larger ears and eyes.

BROWN RAT *Rattus norvegicus*

Brown Rats (also known as Common or Norway Rats) are found almost worldwide as a result of accidental introduction by man. They occur mainly around human settlements, but also in farmland, on sea shores, river banks and on ships. They grow to nearly 50cm (the tail is less than half the total length)

dark phase (below)

brown phase

$\times \frac{3}{4}$ fore

hind

and can weigh over 500gm. Colour varies considerably; the commonest form is brownish above, paler below, but blackish forms are not uncommon. Brown Rats make extensive burrows and are strong swimmers. They are omnivores, and in turn are major prey for animals such as foxes, polecats, cats and owls. They cause extensive damage to stored foods, and their droppings, tooth-marks and general spoliation are characteristic. Up to 5 litters of up to 12 young are produced a year and the offspring mature at about 3 months. Brown Rats are very similar to Black Rats (p. 102) and colour is not a good guide for identification; Brown Rats are larger, with proportionally smaller ears, a blunter muzzle and shorter tail. They are the ancestors of laboratory and other domesticated varieties of rats.

skull

damage to
stored food

HOUSE MOUSE *Mus musculus*

tail
dragged

× I

fore

hind

The House Mouse was originally native to Asia, but has spread to all parts of Europe except a few islands and some of the more remote and uninhabited areas. They are found practically everywhere there is human habitation and there are also populations living in the 'wild', though usually in agricultural areas. House Mice are between 75–100mm long with a tail of about equal length and weigh up to 28gm; those around human habitations are usually larger than the 'wild' ones, with proportionally longer tails. In Iberia and the south of France another species, *M. spretus*, and in s.e. Europe, *M. hortulanus*, occurs. The other forms are also often markedly different in colouring; the ones living in the countryside in western Europe tend to be browner, the town mice more uniform greyish without the pale belly. In eastern Europe both sorts have pale bellies. They will devour anything digestible, spoiling stored foods, and leave a characteristic odour, holes in skirtings, untidy nests, tunnels in ricks, etc. They breed rapidly with litters of 5 or 6, which are weaned at 18 days and mature 6 weeks later; they can produce up to 10 litters a year. They are most likely to be confused with Wood mice (p. 98), which have longer tails, larger eyes and ears and are browner. Young rats (pp. 102–5) have a thicker tail and larger head and feet.

DORMOUSE *Muscardinus avellanarius*

The Dormouse is found in thick woodlands, hedgerows and parklands over most of Europe except Iberia, the south-east and west Balkans, most of Scandinavia, Scotland and Ireland; it is mainly found in deciduous woods, occasionally among conifers and is often associated with hazels and honeysuckle. It grows to around 14cm, of which the thickly furred tail makes up just under half, and its weight varies from 15–40gm. The Dormouse is strictly nocturnal and very arboreal; during the day it sleeps in a roughly globular nest usually built in a dense bush above ground but often in the base of coppicing or among

hazel nuts opened by Dormouse

,roots. These nests are made of twigs, bark, grasses and moss and are about 75mm in diameter; breeding nests are twice the size and often made of honeysuckle bark. Dormice usually have 2 litters a year of 3 or 4 young, occasionally more. They are mainly vegetarian and feed primarily on nuts, fruit and seeds. The presence of Dormice can often be detected by large areas of honeysuckle or other vegetation stripped of bark and foliage. During winter months, Dormice hibernate in a nest, often among leaves at the bottom of a coppice or among roots. Other similar species include other dormice (pp. 110–13), the Harvest Mouse (p. 96) which is much smaller with a thin tail, the Wood Mouse (p. 98) which is a poor climber with an almost unfurred tail, and the Bank Vole (p. 78) which has a short tail and is a much darker colour.

hibernating
Dormouse

FAT DORMOUSE *Glis glis*

The Fat or Edible Dormouse is widely distributed over most of Europe, but is absent from Scandinavia, the Low Countries, northern France and most of Iberia. It occurs on Crete, Corfu, Sicily, Sardinia and Corsica; it has been introduced into Britain and there is now a small thriving population centred on the Chiltern Hills. The Fat Dormouse is found mainly in well-wooded habitats with undergrowth. It is the largest of the European dormice, growing to over 30cm, of which the bushy tail is less than half; it weighs up to 180gm.

opened nuts

Fat Dormice are rather squirrel-like in appearance but have larger eyes. They are mainly nocturnal, but occasionally emerge during the day; they are primarily arboreal and extremely agile. They build their nests (often using beech leaves) in rock clefts, old woodpecker's holes, bird boxes (often leaving distinctive heaps of droppings on the lid), and even in the lofts of houses. They feed on a wide variety of fruits, nuts and insects and can be a pest in orchards and conifer plantations if they are abundant. They are often sociable, with several families living together. In winter they hibernate, often in burrows or even in cellars. Up to 8, though usually 4–5, young are born in midsummer. Fat Dormouse are most likely to be confused with the Garden Dormouse or Forest Dormouse (p. 112) or, in England, with the introduced Grey Squirrel (p. 60) which is larger and often brownish on the back (see below).

Grey Squirrel

Fat Dormouse

DORMICE

Garden Dormouse

Forest Dormouse

Mouse-tailed Dormouse

The top 2 species illustrated opposite are the **Garden Dormouse** (*Eliomys quercinus*), found in much of Europe as far north as the Baltic coast and Finland, and the **Forest Dormouse** (*Dryomys nitedula*), found in the east and south-east of Europe as far north as Moscow. Both species are usually found in woodlands, parks and gardens. The Garden Dormouse grows to a total length of over 25cm, of which the tail is just under half; the Forest Dormouse is slightly smaller; as in all dormice the weight is variable according to the time of year. The 2 species can be distinguished by their facial masks and tails: in the Garden Dormouse the mask extends behind the eye, and the tail is only bushy at the end. Both dormice are largely nocturnal and although often seen on the ground they are excellent climbers. They are omnivores and feed on a wide variety of buds, fruits, nuts, berries and seeds as well as insects, molluscs, bird's eggs and even baby mammals. They build domed nests with an entrance in the side, often using an old bird's nest as a base, and the litter of 3–6 young is weaned at about 1 month old. In winter, they hibernate in holes in trees, buildings, caves and even burrows. Both species are vocal and make a variety of growls, snoring noises, whistles and hisses. They are most likely to be confused with the Fat Dormouse (p. 110) which is larger and has a dark patch only in front of the eyes. The third species illustrated opposite is the **Mouse-tailed Dormouse** *Myomimus roachi*, a little-known species found only in southern Bulgaria.

BIRCH MICE

Steppe Mouse

Northern Birch Mouse

The **Northern Birch Mouse** *Sicista betulina* has a very patchy distribution from Scandinavia, Finland and the western USSR south through Germany, Poland and Czechoslovakia to Romania. It is confined to mountainous areas where it lives in a variety of mainly woodland habitats, but also marshes and even arable land; it is usually found in dense undergrowth, in habitats similar to those of dormice. The Northern Birch Mouse grows to a total length of about

16cm, including a tail of about 10cm. The upper parts are yellowish brown with a conspicuous black band running from the back of the head to the base of the tail. They are very agile, and climb well using the partially prehensile tail. They are mainly nocturnal, and feed mainly on insects, but also on seeds and berries. In summer they build nests in dense vegetation or in holes in stumps and in winter they hibernate in a hole which they excavate. A single litter of 2–6 young is born during the summer. The voice is a high-pitched whistle.

The **Steppe Mouse** or Southern Birch Mouse *S. subtilis* is found in the steppe zones of Asia and southern Russia, extending westwards into Romania with isolated populations in Hungary, Austria and Czechoslovakia. It is found mainly in steppe grasslands, and also occurs in cultivated areas. In general appearance the Steppe Mouse is superficially similar to the Northern Birch Mouse: the body is approximately the same size, but the tail is proportionally shorter; the black band running down the back is bordered with a pale yellowish stripe either side. Its habits are not very well known, but it is probably less nocturnal than the Northern Birch Mouse. Northern Birch Mice and Steppe Mice are most likely to be confused with the Harvest Mouse (p. 96) which is smaller and lacks the dorsal stripe, the Striped Field Mouse (p. 100) which is larger but with a proportionally shorter tail, the Dormouse (p. 108) which lacks the stripe and has a furry tail, or with Wood mice (p. 98), which lack the stripe.

CRESTED PORCUPINE *Hystrix cristata*

Crested Porcupine

The Crested Porcupine's occurrence in Europe is almost certainly as a result of introductions by man; it is found in Italy, Sicily, northern Greece, southern Yugoslavia and Albania in dry open woodland habitats with cover such as undergrowth or boulders, usually in the vicinity of cultivated lands. This unmistakable animal grows to a maximum length of nearly 70cm and has a tail of up to 12cm and weighs up to 15kg; it has a stiff crest on the head and neck and it has long spines – much longer (up to 40cm) than those of hedgehogs – the only other animal with which it could possibly be confused. Porcupines are nocturnal and live in burrows or in rock clefts. A single litter of 2–4 young is born in summer, and the family may stay together sharing the den until the next breeding season; although they become less active in winter they do not hibernate. Porcupines are rodents, and feed mainly on roots, and are often serious pests of agriculture particularly if root crops are grown; they also feed on leaves and stems of plants and bark. Their spines protect them from most predators except man; when threatened they partially roll up and shake the spines and tail, making a distinctive rattling noise. In Britain **Hodgson's Porcupine** *H. hodgsoni* has escaped from a wildlife park and lived and bred ferally for a period; it may possibly get established, in which case it would become a serious pest to agriculture. It is very similar to the Crested Porcupine, but has only a rather short crest on the top of the head and neck.

Hodgson's Porcupine

COYPU *Myocastor coypus*

Originally from southern South America, the Coypu was brought to Europe for fur farming but has escaped, or been introduced, in many parts of Europe, including France, Germany, the Netherlands, the USSR, Scandinavia, parts of eastern Europe and England. It is found in marshes, rivers, lakes and reed beds, is a very good swimmer, dives well and rarely travels far from water. It swims with the head and most of the top of the body visible. The Coypu is one of the largest rodents, growing to a total length of up to about 110cm, of which the tail is just under

$\times \frac{1}{4}$ fore

hind

half; an adult weighs around 9kg. The head is massive, with prominent whiskers and large, orange incisors. Coypu feed mainly on aquatic plants but sometimes come ashore to feed (particularly in hard weather) and may raid crops such as sugar beet (below). The 2–9 young are born in nests usually built above the ground though Coypu also burrow into embankments and may cause extensive damage. The young are active soon after birth and there are usually 2 litters a year. Coypu droppings, often seen on banks and paths in the areas where they occur, are large and distinctive: they are elongated and fairly narrow, 20–40mm long and have lengthwise grooves. The young might be confused with Water voles (p. 80) but otherwise Coypu are most likely to be confused with Musk Rats (p. 82) or Beavers (p. 66).

Coypu-damaged
banks and crops

WOLF *Canis lupus*

Iberian form

×⅓

fore

hind

Wolves were once widespread throughout Europe but have been wiped out in all but a few remote areas: a few occur in Scandinavia, occasionally crossing from the USSR, and small isolated populations survive in the mountains of Spain, Italy and the Balkans. Looking like a large, heavily built dog, the wolf grows to a total length (including the tail) of up to about 150cm, occasionally larger, stand about 70–80cm at the shoulder and weigh up to 72kg, but usually less than 50kg; its colour can be rather variable, but is usually greyish. Wolf packs in Europe usually consist of a she-wolf and her litter of 3–4, and occasionally the previous year's litter. They feed on a variety of animals from mice to Elk. Wolves are fairly vocal, the best known call being the howls used by group members of a pack in winter. Five to six cubs are born in a den in a cave or burrow, and are reared by both parents.

Scandinavian form

GOLDEN JACKAL *Canis aureus*

The Golden Jackal is only found in south-eastern Europe as far north as the USSR, Romania and Hungary. It lives mainly on steppes and in open country with scrub and dense cover and often goes into towns and villages to scavenge; it is rarely found in woods and forests. This jackal looks rather like a small, lean Alsatian (German Shepherd) dog with a shortish tail and comparatively large ears; it grows to a total length of up to about 120cm, of which the tail is around a quarter. Persecution has made it shy and usually nocturnal. It is mainly a scavenger, but occasionally hunts, often in pairs or family groups, taking sheep, goats, and poultry as well as small wild animals; it also eats a wide variety of invertebrates including locusts in summer and also fruit in autumn. Its voice is a high-pitched penetrating howl, often taken up by more than one jackal, and can be heard at dusk at all times of the year; the footprints and scats are virtually indistinguishable from those of dogs. Jackals breed in burrows, usually in dense cover, often utilising an old Badger set or Red Fox's earth. They normally have 4 or 5 cubs in a litter; the cubs are cared for by both parents and become independent at about 6 months. The Golden Jackal is most likely to be confused with the closely related Wolf (p. 120) which is larger and greyer, the Red Fox (p. 126), which is redder with a long tail, and the domestic dog; all 3 are illustrated below.

Wolf

domestic dog

Golden Jackal

ARCTIC FOX *Alopex lagopus*

summer pelage

winter pelage

This fox occurs widely in the Arctic, usually above the treeline; it is also found on most northern islands including Iceland, Spitzbergen, Bear Island, Novaya Zemlya, Franz Josef Land and Svalard. In winter it may wander southwards, often covering long distances. It is also kept on fur farms in other parts of Europe and may occasionally escape. It grows to about 90cm in length, of which about one third is tail; and to a height of about 30cm at the shoulder. Arctic Foxes exhibit 2 distinct colour phases which often occur side by side; in one the fur is brownish above and pale below in summer, and turns white in winter; in the other, less common variety, it is brownish grey in summer and bluish grey in winter. Living in the Arctic, they are active by day and night; they make extensive dens, either by digging, or by using natural fissures in rocks. They are often very sociable, with several families living close together and forming large, loosely organised packs during the winter months. Arctic Foxes have 2 litters a year, of up to 6 cubs, depending on the availability of food. They are opportunist feeders, hunting and scavenging on a variety of animals including voles, lemmings and seabirds, feeding on the remains of Polar Bears' kills, and eating berries in summer; they make caches of surplus food. The footprints and scats are similar to those of a small fox. The Arctic Fox is unlikely to be confused with any other species except possibly a small fox or dog; it can be recognised by its rather short muzzle and rounded ears.

RED FOX *Vulpes vulpes*

Widespread throughout Europe, the Red Fox is the most abundant of the large carnivores and occurs in a wide variety of habitats, but usually in places with cover; in many areas it goes into villages and even lives in towns. Dog-like in appearance with distinctive pointed ears, a narrow muzzle and a bushy, white-tipped tail, the Red Fox measures about 120cm in length, one third of which may be tail, has a shoulder height of up to 40cm and

hind

weighs up to 10kg; its colour is variable but usually rich reddish brown above and white below. Its food consists mainly of rodents but a variety of larger animals and soft fruit are also eaten; animals living in towns scavenge and are often mangy. Litters of 3–8 cubs are born in an underground earth. The presence of a Red Fox can be detected by its purposeful tracks which do not normally wander and pause like those of a domestic dog; the scattered remains of food around its den; a distinctive musty smell; and long, twisted droppings containing hair, bone and insect remains. A variety of yaps and barks or the vixen's (female) bloodcurdling scream may be heard, especially in winter. The Red Fox is the main carrier of rabies in Europe; it is most likely to be confused with the domestic dog, Golden Jackal (p. 122) or Arctic Fox (p. 124).

RACCOON-LIKE DOG
Nyctereutes procyonoides

Like those of the superficially similar Raccoon, the European populations of the Raccoon-like Dog are descended from animals which have been introduced. They were originally from the Far East and in the 1920s they were reared extensively on fur farms in the USSR. Escaped animals soon became established and have now spread westwards colonising much of eastern and northern Europe, including parts of Finland, Sweden, Norway, Germany, Poland, Czechoslovakia, Romania and Hungary. Their favourite habitat is open deciduous woodland with thick undergrowth, usually close to water, but they also occur in a very wide variety of other habitats including coniferous forests. The Raccoon-like Dog is approximately the same size as the Red Fox, but stockier with a more shaggy appearance; it grows to about 80cm long, including a short bushy tail of about 15cm. They feed on a wide variety of small animals, including voles and mice, dung beetles, water beetles, crickets, ground-nesting birds, snakes, baby tortoises, frogs, fish and a wide range of berries, fruits and plants. They are mainly active during twilight and at night; during the day their den is usually in a rock cleft, burrow or in dense vegetation; sometimes they excavate their own burrow, up to 2m deep, with 2 or more entrances. There are usually 6 or 7 cubs in a litter (occasionally up to 16) which are born in early summer. Both parents look after the cubs, which may remain together until winter when they hibernate. The Raccoon-like Dog's tracks are rather neat and round with the 4 toe-prints evenly spread around the front half of the paw and the claw prints visible; they are easily distinguishable from those of foxes (pp. 124–7), dogs and Raccoons (p. 132). The Raccoon-like Dog's facial pattern and shape is superficially similar to that of the unrelated Raccoon which is more agile and has a long, distinctively banded tail.

× ¼
fore

hind

129

BEARS

Polar Bear

Brown Bear

The **Brown Bear** *Ursus arctos* is, or was, found throughout the northern hemisphere. It was once fairly common, but is now rare or extinct over most of Europe and only found in small numbers in Cantabria, the Pyrenees, the Italian Alps and Abruzzi; in Scandinavia, eastern Europe and the Balkan countries it is slightly more numerous. The **Polar Bear** *Thalarctos maritimus* is really a marine species, living on Arctic ice floes and only rarely coming to land (except Arctic islands); the occasional wanderer may reach Iceland, Arctic Norway or the USSR. They were once threatened with extinction, but are now recovering under international protection. Both bears have a body length of up to 2.5m; the females are smaller than the males. The Polar Bear is a larger animal generally, but there is enormous variation in Brown Bears: a large male Brown Bear stands about 1m at the shoulder and weighs up to 265kg; a Polar Bear stands up to 1.4m and weighs up to 450kg. The colour of the Brown Bear is also variable – from almost chocolate brown to pale fawn; the typical colour is sandy brown. Polar Bears are white, though they have a yellowish tinge. Both species are normally solitary. The Brown Bear was once found widely in deciduous woodlands, but has become increasingly restricted to coniferous forests and mountain areas. It is an omnivore, eating berries, nuts and a wide variety of other plant matter as well as carrion, small mammals, insects, honey and occasionally domestic livestock. The tiny (less than 500gm at birth) cubs (usually 3, but can be up to 6) are born in the winter den in January or February. The cubs leave the den with the mother at about 4 months and forage with her, but do not become independent until their second summer. Brown Bears hibernate for at least part of the winter. Polar Bears are strictly carnivorous, usually have only 1 cub, and normally only the female hibernates. Bears are not likely to be confused with any other animal to be found in Europe.

Brown
Bear
$\times \frac{1}{12}$
fore

hind

131

RACCOON   *Procyon lotor*

Originally from North America, the Raccoon was brought to Europe for fur farms, and as a result of a few escapes has now become firmly established. It has spread principally from 2 centres – the Mosel Valley and Eifel district of Germany, and nearby parts of the Netherlands, Luxembourg and France, and also parts of Russia; it is now widespread particularly in Germany. The Raccoon is very adaptable and occurs in a wide variety of habitats, usually in fairly well-wooded country, often near water. But it also occurs in many other habitats, and may live close to man. The Raccoon grows to about 1m long, of which the tail is nearly a third; it weighs up to about 15kg. The most distinctive features are the banded tail and the black facial pattern – often described as a 'robber's mask'. Raccoons are active and intelligent and they are mainly nocturnal; they are excellent climbers and can use their fore-paws as 'hands'. Their habit of sometimes washing their food has given them their French, German (and Latin) names of *Raton laveur* and *Waschbär*. Raccoons are carnivores, though they eat an extremely wide variety of foods, depending on availability; they take molluscs, freshwater crayfish, fish, frogs, insects, birds and their eggs, small mammals, as well as carrion and a wide range of plants, their fruits and seeds; they also often scavenge around human habitations. A den is usually made in a hollow tree, rock cleft or an old burrow of another animal. There are usually 4 cubs in a litter, born in spring; they stay with the mother until the end of the following winter. During the winter months Raccoons may lie up in their dens, but do not actually hibernate. They may be confused with the Raccoon-like Dog (p. 128).

$\times \frac{1}{4}$

fore

hind

133

STOAT AND WEASEL

Stoat
winter pelage
(Ermine)

Stoat
summer
pelage

Weasel

both $\times \frac{3}{4}$

Stoat, fore

hind

Weasel, fore

hind

The **Stoat** (*Mustela erminea*) is found over most of Europe except the southern parts; the **Weasel** (*M. nivalis*) is even more widely distributed but is absent from Ireland. Both species are found right into the Arctic. They occur in a wide variety of habitats, usually in or near woodlands. The Stoat is the larger of the 2 species and the males grow to about 30cm plus another 10cm of tail. Male Weasels are only just over 20cm in length plus a 6cm tail; females are smaller in both species. Male Stoats weigh up to 300gm, male Weasels up to 130gm, the females proportionally less – a female Weasel can weigh under 45gm. However, size is not always a good guide to identification as there is considerable variation and overlap between the 2 species and it is safer to remember that the Stoat has a proportionally longer tail with a black tip and an uneven demarcation between its pale belly and brownish upperparts. Both species turn white in winter in the more northerly and higher parts of their range but Weasels rarely change into winter pelage in Britain. Both species can sometimes be seen hunting rabbits, rats, birds or other animals, often larger than themselves, during the day but they are mainly nocturnal animals. The Stoat has 1 litter per year of about 5 kittens; the Weasel 2 litters. Both species make a variety of hissing, spitting and screaming noises.

MINK

European Mink

American Mink

The **European Mink** *Mustela lutreola* and **American Mink** *M. vison* are closely related and are often thought to be the same species. The European Mink is found mainly in Scandinavia and eastern Europe, though also in western France, but its range is contracting. In contrast, the introduced American Mink has colonised many parts of Europe, including a large part of the British Isles and Scandinavia, where it is now one of the commonest carnivores. Both species are found in a wide range of habitats, normally

×½
fore

hind

fairly near to water, and have long, slender bodies with a bushy tail. The American Mink measures up to 60cm in length, of which just under a third is tail, and a large male weighs over 1kg; the European Mink is on average 50mm smaller and weighs up to 800gm. In both species females are smaller. The European Mink has uniform dark brown fur, with white on the upper and lower lips; the American lacks the white on the upper lip and although usually dark brown it can be a variety of colours, as bred on fur farms. Feeding and general habits are extremely variable: fish, mice, voles, frogs, poultry and waterfowl are all eaten as the opportunity arises; they swim well and climb; they are not particularly vocal but utter high-pitched whistles; and both species usually have litters of from 3–7 young. Mink could be confused with the Otter (p. 146), polecats (pp. 138–41) or possibly the Coypu (p. 118). Mink spraints can be distinguished from those of Otters by an unpleasant 'fishy' smell.

Otter

Mink

POLECATS

European Polecat

The **European Polecat** *Mustela putorius*, although much reduced in numbers and range, occurs throughout most of Europe except the southern Balkans, most Mediterranean islands, Scandinavia and most of the British Isles. At one time it was widespread in Britain, but it was reduced to a few populations in Wales, which are now spreading again. In mainland Europe many polecat populations are continuing to decline. Both the **Steppe Polecat** *M. eversmanni*

$\times \frac{1}{2}$
fore

hind

and the **Marbled Polecat** *Vormela peregusna* are restricted to eastern Europe. The **Ferret** *M. furo* is a domesticated form, but its precise ancestry is unknown. Used for rabbit hunting, they often escape to the wild, and are established on Sicily and Sardinia. Polecats are found in a wide range of habitats, usually fairly wooded, often near human habitations; the Steppe Polecat is found mainly in open country, and the Marbled Polecat in dry and often rocky habitats. The European Polecat grows to about 60cm of which the tail makes up about one third, and weighs 500–1,200gm. Both the Steppe and the Marbled Polecats are slightly smaller; female polecats are smaller than the males. The Ferret varies in colour from creamy white, with pink eyes, to being almost identical to the European Polecat.

Steppe Polecat

Marbled Polecat

European Polecats have a reputation as killers of poultry (*poule chat* or 'chicken cat' in French), but they feed on a wide variety of animals, including rabbits, game birds, rats, mice, frogs and and insects; and they often tackle prey larger than themselves. If they get into a poultry run they can do extensive damage, killing more than they can eat. Polecats mark their territory with the strong smelling fluid from the anal glands; this fluid can also be ejected at intruders, hence an alternative name – foulemart. Although mainly terrestrial, they are good climbers and can swim. They spend much of their time hunting in burrows and tunnels; when hunting they creep with the body stretched out, and the belly almost touching the ground. Four to six kittens are born in late spring or early summer, in a nest in a rabbit warren or other suitable hole, sometimes dug by the parents; the kittens become independent at about 3 months old. Polecats are fairly vocal, making chattering and growling noises when alarmed, also making various hissing and squealing noises; the Steppe Polecat apparently makes a barking noise. The 3 species of polecat are best distinguished from each other by their colouring. They are only likely to be confused with Stoats (p. 134) which are smaller, more slender and redder; martens (p. 142) which are larger, longer legged, and have pale throats; or mink (p. 136) which have more uniform, darker coloration.

'Fitch' Ferret
(wild-coloured
domestic form)

Ferret

MARTENS

Pine Marten

The **Pine Marten** *Martes martes* is widespread over most of northern and central Europe, but absent from much of Spain and the southern Balkans; it occurs in Corsica, Sardinia, Sicily and the British Isles. The **Beech** or **Stone Marten** *M. foina* has a more southerly distribution, including Corfu, Crete and Rhodes, and is missing from the British Isles and northern Europe. The **Sable** *M. zibellina* was formerly found from northern Scandinavia eastwards, but was exterminated

fore

hind

by fur trappers. A programme of conservation and reintroduction in the USSR has been carried out and in the future the Sable may recolonise parts of Europe. The Pine Marten is found mainly in coniferous or mixed woodlands. The Beech Marten is also found in wooded areas, but being more southerly, is more often found in fairly open, rocky habitats; it occasionally comes into villages and even towns. The Pine Martin grows to a length of about 75cm, of which the tail is about one third; the Beech Marten is approximately the same size but more heavily built, the Sable slightly smaller. Both martens feed on small animals; in spring 2–6 kittens are born. Martens are only likely to be confused with polecats (p. 138) which are smaller, less agile, and lack a pale throat patch.

Beech Marten

Sable

WOLVERINE *Gulo gulo*

The Wolverine or Glutton was once found throughout the northern hemisphere taiga zones and, in summer, in tundra as well and occasionally much further south. It is now endangered in Europe and is only found in small numbers in Norway, Sweden, Finland and the USSR. The Wolverine is a large rather bear-like animal, related to the Weasel and Stoat, growing to a length of about 80cm with an additional 12–15cm of bushy tail, and weighing up to 30kg, although there is considerable variation depending on the time of year. Its footprints are characteristic as its feet are large and covered with hair, enabling it to run on firm snow and so giving it

fore $\times\frac{1}{3}$

hind

a considerable advantage when chasing animals with hooves. Wolverines eat a wide variety of animals and plants, hunting animals up to the size of Reindeer and Elk when the opportunity arises, driving Lynx, foxes and wolves away from their prey and also eating carrion. Although normally solitary, the range of the male and female will sometimes overlap; they mark their territory by biting chunks out of tree trunks and depositing scent. A litter of 2–3 young is born in February or March in a den underground, among boulders or excavated in a snowdrift. The Wolverine in unlikely to be confused with any other species in its range.

OTTER *Lutra lutra*

The Otter is found close to water throughout Europe and northern Asia; it was once widespread and abundant but it has declined rapidly since the beginning of the century and is now considered endangered in most parts of Europe. It grows to about 130cm including the tail, which makes up a third of the total length, weighs up to 15kg and is usually a rich brownish colour with a whitish or greyish

spraints on rocks

fore

hind

throat and belly. On land its large tail, thick at the base and tapering to the tip, is characteristic; while in water often all that is seen is the flattened head with a broad muzzle, or, if the Otter is diving, a trail of bubbles (from the air trapped in the fur). Otters are powerful swimmers, using the tail, and can dive for over 5 minutes. Due to centuries of persecution the Otter is mainly nocturnal; however, it can be detected from signs such as half-eaten fish, sweet-smelling droppings (spraints) which they usually deposit on landmarks such as the base of a bridge, and slides which it makes in mud or snow on river banks. Otters breed at any time of the year. It may be confused with mink (p. 136) which are smaller, and aquatic rodents such as Coypu (p. 118), which lack the large tail and have smaller heads.

young on winter slide

adult swimming

BADGER *Meles meles*

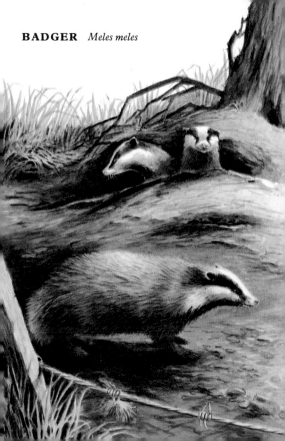

The Badger is widely distributed and found in most parts of Europe except northern and western Scandinavia and the highlands of Scotland; it is found in Crete, Ireland and the Balearics. Although widely distributed it is often rather scarce due to persecution. It lives in a wide variety of habitats, but mainly deciduous and mixed woods, and Mediterranean scrublands as well as more open countryside. A Badger is about the size of a medium-sized dog, standing about 30cm at the shoulder and up to about 70cm long and weighing up to 22kg; it has an extremely distinctive pattern and is unlikely to be confused with any other European animal. Badgers excavate extensive burrows (sets), around which signs of activity such as 'scratching trees' and latrine pits can be found. In many areas Badgers are almost exclusively nocturnal and very shy, but where they are not persecuted they often emerge by day. They feed mainly on small invertebrates, but are opportunists and will eat a wide variety of animal and vegetable matter including carrion. The young are born underground in late winter and first venture out after about 2 months, when they are very playful. When moving from the set to the feeding ground badgers use well worn tracks, which often look like human footpaths – but go *under* logs and other obstacles. They move with a bouncing gait.

$\times \frac{1}{3}$
fore

hind

GENET *Genetta genetta*

The Genet is found in well-wooded, often fairly marshy areas in southern and western France, Iberia and on the island of Majorca; it was formerly more widespread, occurring as far east as Belgium and the Jura in Germany, but has become increasingly local and rare and has disappeared from many parts of its former range. It is likely that it was originally introduced from north Africa, where it is widespread from Morocco to Cyrenaica; it is also found in savannah south of the Sahara. The Genet is about the size of a domestic cat, but with short legs, standing up to 20cm at the shoulder and weighing around 2kg; its total length is around 100cm, of which the tapering banded tail is nearly half, giving it a much more slender appearance than a cat. It is an extremely shy and elusive animal and very little is known about its habits in Europe. It is very agile and not only climbs and jumps well but also swims; it is mainly carnivorous but also feeds on a variety of fruits and berries. The 2–3 kittens are born in spring in a hollow tree or among rocks. The Genet is most likely to be confused with the Mongoose (p. 152), which is only found in southern Iberia and Yugoslavia, lacks spots and is much larger, the Wild Cat (p. 154), which is longer legged with a more striped pattern, or feral cat (p. 155), which normally has a much more slender tail and is always longer legged with a shorter muzzle.

MONGOOSE *Herpestes ichneumon*

This species of Mongoose is widely distributed in Africa. In Europe they are found only in Spain, where they were almost certainly introduced, and Italy and Yugoslavia, where they are known to have been introduced. In Spain, although formerly widespread, they are more or less restricted to the area around the Sierra Morena in the south. They are most often found in scrub and other areas with dense undergrowth, including marshes and swamps. This species of Mongoose is comparatively large – with a body of up to 55cm and a tail of up to 45cm; it weighs up to 8kg. In general appearance it is rather marten-like, but with a long tapering tail. Mongooses are rarely seen, though they are only partially nocturnal. They hunt either singly or in small groups, feeding on a wide variety of small mammals (up to the size of rabbits), reptiles, fish and other animals; they also raid chicken runs and are consequently persecuted. They take large numbers of reptiles including snakes and also eggs, which they smash on rocks. There are 2–4 kittens in a litter, and when the young leave the nest they follow the mother in a 'caravan', each one with its head tucked under the tail of its predecessor. The Mongoose is most likely to be confused with martens (p. 142), which have bushier tails and longer legs, or the Genet (p. 150), which has distinctive spotting and larger ears. Another species, *H. edwardsi*, has been introduced in Italy.

WILD CAT *Felis silvestris*

Sardinian

Scottish

Formerly more widespread, the Wild Cat is patchily distributed over much of Iberia, Italy and the Balkans, with isolated populations in Scotland, France, Germany and most larger Mediterranean islands. It is found mainly in woodlands with open clearings. Although there are probably very few pure bred Wild Cats left now, they are larger than domestic cats, growing to a maximum length of about 130cm, of which the tail is over one third, and standing up to 40cm at the shoulder; the weight is 5–10kg (maxi-

×⅖
fore

hind

mum 15kg). They are distinguished from domestic cats by a larger size, a proportionally shorter, bushier, blunt-tipped tail and also by pale paws and a brownish nose. Wild Cats are active mainly at night and during twilight; they are very agile, but although good climbers, mainly terrestrial. They depend on stealth to catch their prey of rabbits, voles and other mammals up to the size of Roe Deer fawns and lambs; they also eat carrion. Wild Cats are often vocal and their calls are similar to those of domestic cats. One to eight kittens are born in a den in a rock cleft or hollow tree. They are independent at 3–4 months. The Wild Cat is most likely to be confused with domestic cats (see above); Genet (p. 150); or Lynx (p. 156).

feral cats

LYNX *Felis lynx*

Lynx

The Lynx was once widespread throughout most of mainland Europe in taiga and mountain forest habitats. It is now extinct in most parts of Europe and there are only remnant populations in Iberia, Scandinavia, eastern and south-eastern Europe; however, there are programmes to reintroduce Lynx into parts of their former range in Switzerland, Germany and other parts of central Europe. The Lynx is a large cat and grows to between 80 and 130cm long with a short tail of not more than about 25cm. It has long legs, distinctive ear tufts, and a stumpy black-tipped tail. The markings are very variable, but the base colour is usually sandy with at least some spotting, though in the north and east of the range the spotting is often indistinct; in Iberia, they are normally clearly spotted, and in east and south-east Europe the markings are variable. The spotted forms are sometimes known as Pardel Lynx and were once thought to be a separate species; they interbreed freely with unspotted forms. Lynx are normally solitary and mainly nocturnal; they feed primarily on rodents, rabbits and hares, young deer and domestic animals, and ground-dwelling birds. A single litter normally of 2 or 3 young (kittens) is born in summer, in a lair in a hollow tree, rock cleft or similar site; the kittens remain with the mother until the following year. Lynx make a variety of hissing and chattering sounds and in the breeding season the male has a high pitched call which ends in a softer moan. Lynx are not likely to be confused with any other species except the Wild Cat (p. 154), which is smaller, with a long, thick, striped tail.

Pardel Lynx

WALRUS *Odobenus rosmarus*

The Walrus is a coastal species found in the north Atlantic, Pacific and Arctic Oceans. Its distribution is now patchy: in Europe it is normally only found off Norway and Russia, and is a vagrant elsewhere. It is the largest seal occurring in European waters, the males growing up to 4.5m, females up to 3m; a large bull can weigh over 2 tonnes. Both sexes are similar in colour, usually yellowish brown, but may be slightly reddish. Apart from its enormous size, the most distinctive features of the Walrus are its tusks which are larger (up to 70cm) in males. Other characteristics are the 'moustache' of bristles on the snout; the hind feet which, unlike those of other European seals, can be turned forwards; and the thick, loose, wrinkled skin. Juveniles are darker, with smaller tusks (less than 3cm long at 1 year old). Females breed alternate years, in colonies, which are often very dense. They feed extensively on bivalve molluscs, diving for up to 10 minutes to depths of down to about 30m. They are vocal, making a variety of noises: the most common is between the mooing of a cow and a rather deep dog bark, repeated several times. The Walrus is unlikely to be mistaken for any other seal because of its size and its tusks.

COMMON SEAL *Phoca vitulina*

male

female

pup

The Common or Harbour Seal is widely distributed around the coasts of most of the northern hemisphere; in Europe it is found from the Atlantic coast of northern Portugal northwards to the Arctic. It is normally found in inshore waters, and often occurs in sea lochs, in fjords and even up rivers. Common Seals are one of the smaller seals, growing up to between 1.5–2m and weighing between 50–150kg. The basic colour is very variable, but usually greyish or greyish yellow, with dense mottling; the whiskers are white. The Common Seal has a rather short, rounded head, with a profile which is more concave than that of the Grey Seal. When only the head can be seen, the angled nostrils, with the bases nearly meeting, are characteristic. The pups are born in spring or early summer with grey fur, having already moulted their white coats at birth; they are very well developed and able to swim. They are about 80cm long and weigh around 10kg. The pups are born on beaches and sand bars and suckled in the sea. After 3 or 4 weeks they are no longer suckled by the mother and feed like adults on a wide variety of coastal marine life, including fish, cephalopods, shellfish and crustaceans. The Common Seal is comparatively silent, but during the mating season, in autumn, a variety of barking noises are made as the seals perform the 'aquabatics' which accompany mating. They leap out of the water, blow out air noisily as they submerge, and roll around in pairs, splashing violently. Common Seals may be confused with the Grey Seal (p. 166), which is often more abundant.

RINGED SEAL   *Phoca hispida*

female

pup

The Ringed Seal is one of the more numerous species of seal and is found throughout the Arctic Ocean, wherever the water is open; it also occurs in the northern parts of the Baltic Sea, and the Gulf of Bothnia. Isolated populations occur in fresh water in Lake Saimaa (Finland), which is over 60m above sea level, and Lake Ladoga in Russia. Vagrants occur south to Iceland, the British Isles and other parts of north-west Europe. The Ringed Seal grows to 1.2–1.85m and weighs up to 110kg. The fur colour is blackish, with pale ring markings which become brown by autumn. The markings are variable: in some they are so numerous as to touch and join up, in others so thin as to be obliterated by the dark centres. The white or yellowish pups are born in March or April. Ringed Seals make breathing holes in the ice and dive for up to 20 minutes; they live in small groups, or are solitary. They are most likely to be confused with the Common Seal (p. 160) which has a spotted underside.

BEARDED SEAL *Erignathus barbatus*

The Bearded Seal is found throughout the Arctic Ocean, breeding as far south as the northern coasts of Norway and the USSR; they migrate southwards in winter, and are occasionally seen as far south as Britain and France. It is one of the largest seals in European waters, growing to 2.2–3.1m and weighing up to 400kg; the females are smaller than the males. The upper parts are uniformly dark greyish or brownish, occasionally with indistinct spots, the underparts paler; the most distinctive features are the long, curving vibrissae (whiskers) which curl at the ends when they are dry. Bearded seals are generally solitary and live around the edge of the ice. The dark grey pups are normally born in late winter or early spring; after about 2 weeks they moult into a bluish grey coat. The Bearded Seal is very similar to the Grey Seal (p. 166), but the latter lacks the distinctive whiskers and is not as uniformly coloured.

male with
dry whiskers

HARP SEAL *Pagophilus groenlandicus*

female

pup

The Harp or Greenland Seal is a polar species living in the northern oceans, from North Baffin Island eastwards to the White Sea. It is only rarely found further south than 60° north in European waters and has been occasionally seen off Britain, Ireland, the Netherlands, Germany, Norway and Denmark. It is a smallish seal; bulls grow to about 2.2m from head to tail; cows less than 1.5m. Viewed from the side, male Harp Seals have an unmistakable contrasting pattern which can be said to look like a harp; the female is greyer above and yellow below, with dark blotches along the sides instead of the bands; juveniles are brownish with dark spots. Adults breed in spring on icefields, often in enormous herds. The pups are white at birth, and acquire the adult pelage over 5 years. The Canadian population is thought to have declined from over 6 million to around 1¼ million, as a result of commercial sealers. It is unlikely to be mistaken for any other seal.

HOODED SEAL *Cystophora cristata*

The Hooded or Bladder-nose Seal occurs in summer on the edge of the drift ice in the Arctic Ocean; in winter it moves further south and vagrants have been recorded as far south as Britain and the Bay of Biscay. It grows to 2–2.35m and weighs up to 400kg; the females are only slightly smaller than the males. The upperside is bluish grey with variable paler markings; the females are generally paler. The male has an inflatable 'hood' on the nose and top of the head. The single pup is born in spring, and is silvery blue above contrasting with light cream fur underneath. Hooded Seals are often found with Harp Seals, but occur in smaller herds than the Harp Seal. Hooded Seals are most likely to be confused with Grey Seals (p. 166), which have a more tapering muzzle and dark spotting.

male

female

pup

GREY SEAL *Halichoerus grypus*

male

female

pup

male

female

The Grey Seal is a mostly coastal species, occurring in 3 separate, and apparently isolated, populations in the eastern Atlantic (around Newfoundland, north-western Europe and the Baltic). The largest breeding colonies are around Britain, but it also breeds, or has bred, on most European coasts north of northern France; it is a rare visitor to the coasts of northern Spain and Portugal. The Grey Seal is one of the largest European species of seal with bulls growing up to 3m in length, but usually about 2.3m from head to tail; mature cows usually average around 2m. A mature bull weighs up to about 200kg. The coloration is extremely variable and confusing. The male usually has light patches on a generally dark background, while the female is generally lighter with fewer dark markings. As moult approaches the pattern becomes less distinct, particularly when the seals are hauled out and the pelt is dry. Pups are white at birth, and begin to moult at about 10 days old when they start to acquire a coat with similar markings to that of adults. Grey Seals breed in autumn in small colonies, mostly on rocky coasts and islands. They haul out on land to rest, but also sleep vertically in water, showing the head with a characteristic profile which distinguishes it readily from the Common Seal (p. 160) – the only other widespread species which is found within its range. The Grey Seal is highly vocal, particularly the cows which make a high-pitched hooting when they are on the breeding beaches.

MONK SEAL *Monachus monachus*

male

female

pup

The Monk Seal is the only seal normally found in the Mediterranean and the adjacent warm waters of the Atlantic. Due to persecution by fishermen it is now found only in very small scattered colonies principally in the Aegean Sea, and now only rarely in the Black Sea, around the Balearics, Sardinia and Sicily; the total population (including those outside Europe) is probably less than 1,000 animals and it is now classified as an endangered species. The surviving Monk Seals are very shy and rarely seen; they are mainly coastal, living in isolated, usually rocky, coves and often breed in sea caves. Adults grow to a total length of about 2.5m and weigh over 320kg. Their upperparts are dark grey or brownish and the underparts cream or whitish; the females and young animals are generally paler than adult males and some old animals become whitish. Comparatively little is known about the habits of the Monk Seal. The young are born in October or November and are about 1m long at birth; the cows mate alternate years and the young are believed to remain with the mother for up to 3 years. Monk Seals make a variety of dog-like yelps and barks, as well as other noises variously described as sneezing and howling, and also sharp repetitive calls. The only seals which are likely to be encountered within the range of the Monk Seal are the Common Seal (p. 160), which is much smaller and spotted on the upperparts, and the Grey Seal (p. 166), which has a large, rather pointed snout and is spotted or blotched on the upperparts.

FERAL HORSES *Equus ferus*

Exmoor Pony

Wild Horses or Tarpans became extinct in Europe – in Poland and the Ukraine – in the 19th century. However, there are still primitive breeds of horses in many parts of Europe – there is no difference between a horse and a pony: the latter usually refers to the smaller breeds. Feral Horses are usually found in moorlands and other marginal lands, although originally Wild Horses occurred in open woodlands as well. In Britain they are found in the New Forest, on Dartmoor, Bodmin Moor and Exmoor; there are also other ancient breeds, such as Shetlands, but all of them are increasingly domesticated, and, although they roam freely, they are generally rounded up at least once a year. These horses are generally fairly dark chestnuts, bays or browns although their colour varies considerably. Other more or less domesticated horses are found in the Camargue on the Rhône Delta in southern France; these are larger, grey when young and usually white when older. The Fjord Pony, which has a short mane like its wild ancestors, is found in Norway, and other primitive breeds in Germany, Iceland, Gotland and Ireland; a herd of Tarpan-like horses based on the Polish Konik horse has been bred and now lives in a semi-wild state in Poland. The African Ass *E. asinus* is also found in Europe, but only as a domestic animal. Mules are hybrids (usually sterile) between asses and horses.

Fjord Pony

WILD BOAR *Sus scrofa*

female with young

The Wild Boar is the ancestor of the domestic pig and was once very widespread throughout Europe and Asia. It is now extinct or very much reduced in most parts of Europe; it is extinct in Britain and Fenno-Scandinavia; it occurs on Sardinia and Corsica. Although the Wild Boar has disappeared from most of the more populous parts of Europe it has also been preserved (and reintroduced) as a game animal in many areas. They occur in a wide variety of habitats but prefer mixed woodlands, with marshes or arable lands (where they often cause considerable damage). Wild Boar are large, growing to 1–1.5m long, and standing up to 90cm at the shoulder. The weight is very variable, but a full grown boar (male) can weigh up to 175kg, a sow (female) up to 150kg. In eastern Europe they can be even larger and heavier. Wild Boar are heavily built, usually dark coloured, with thick bristly hair. Occasionally interbreeds with domestic pigs and intermediate colours and 'balding' animals occur. Both sexes have tusks, which are often quite large in the males. Wild Boar are normally solitary, but females are often accompanied by their young. They are mainly nocturnal, lying up in a lair under a fallen tree or rock; there are normally several lairs within a boar's territory. The male joins the female (and her litter) during the rut, which occurs in midwinter, for several weeks, after which he returns to his solitary life. The litter of 2–10 piglets is born in spring. They have longitudinal brown and yellowish stripes and are active a few days after birth. Has been re-introduced into Sweden and Norway.

× ¼
fore

hind

173

DEER

Introduction

Deer are hoofed animals and in Europe vary in size from the tiny Muntjac to the Elk. Because they have been traditional quarry species in most of Europe, a specialised vocabulary for describing the native deer and their habits has developed in most languages.

Antlers	The horns, which are carried by the male of all species except the Chinese Water Deer, and also by female Reindeer. They are shed after the breeding season.
Buck	Male Fallow, Roe and Muntjac.
Bull	Male Elk.
Calf	Young Reindeer and Elk.
Cow	Female Elk.
Crotties	Droppings.
Doe	Female Fallow and Roe Deer.
Elk	American name for Wapiti – the equivalent of Red Deer.
Fawn	Young Fallow Deer.
Fraying Stock	A tree rubbed by deer's antlers to remove velvet – see opposite.
Hind	Female Red Deer.
Moose	American name for Elk.
Rut	The breeding season of deer.
Slot	Hoofprints.
Stag	Male Red Deer.
Target	The rump patch.

MUNTJAC *Muntiacus reevesi*

adult male

Originally from southern China and Taiwan, the Muntjac has been introduced, or escaped, in southern England, where it is now widespread, and in France. They are found in well-wooded habitats with dense cover including young forestry plantations, overgrown gardens (even in the outskirts of towns), gorse and bramble thickets. They are the smallest deer found in Europe, standing up to 46cm at the shoulder, and weighing up to about 15kg.

During the summer they are a rich chestnut above, in winter duller brown-grey. The male has short (maximum 75mm) antlers, and enlarged canine teeth (up to 40mm). The young (fawns), have spots in lines and are born at any time of the year. Muntjac appear to live in family groups, usually consisting of a buck (male), doe (female), juvenile and fawn. The droppings are used in marking territory and they are black and shiny, usually with a pimple at one end and a depression at the other. The Muntjac is most likely to be confused with Chinese Water Deer (p. 190), which never has antlers, carries its head higher and lacks the angular back of the Muntjac; Roe Deer (p. 192), which has longer antlers in the buck, an almost insignificant tail but a distinct white rump patch, and is larger. The Muntjac might also be confused with a Red Fox (p. 126) or dog, but these have long tails.

× 4/5

nd   fore-
ot   foot

droppings

fleeing female
showing flash

177

FALLOW DEER *Cervus dama*

stag

doe

albino doe

fawn

male ×½

female ×⅓

The Fallow Deer was originally found mainly in deciduous woodland areas around the Mediterranean, but has been introduced into many parts of Europe and the rest of the world. They are usually found in well-wooded habitats, with thick undergrowth. Completely wild herds are very secretive and usually nocturnal. Adult males are about 170cm long and 90cm at the shoulders, and weigh up to 90kg; females are slightly smaller. The colour is variable, particularly in park and wild herds. Typically they are a rich reddish brown above with prominent white spots, and pale below, with a clear whitish stripe along the sides; in winter the spots are lost (except in the 'menil' variety) and the colour is greyer. Colour varieties range from almost entirely blackish to pure white. The most characteristic feature of the male is the palmate antlers. The target (rump pattern) shows a relatively long, black-tipped white tail and a black edge to the top of the rump. For most of the year the mature males usually live in bachelor herds. The rut commences in late autumn when males take possession of their harems. The males make a deep, loud belching call during the rut. The single fawn is born in early summer, and spends much of its time alone, hidden among vegetation. It is most likely to be confused with the Red Deer (p. 184) or the Sika Deer (p. 180).

SIKA DEER *Cervus nippon*

summer

hind

stag

The Sika Deer is a native of eastern Asia which has been introduced into Europe and is now well established in Ireland, Britain, Denmark and central and eastern Europe, where it shows a preference for fairly well-wooded habitats. It stands up to about 85cm at the shoulder, is 120cm long and weighs up to 55kg; the female is slightly smaller. The upperparts are reddish brown, usually with spotting in summer,

×½

but uniform in winter; the tail is short and almost hidden. The stags carry relatively small antlers, with up to eight points; they fray in August and the rut is in the autumn, when the male develops a shaggy mane on the throat and marks and defends his territory. The rutting call is a whistle which develops into a roar as the rut progresses; other calls can be likened to blowing a 'raspberry' and that made by blowing over a blade of grass. The spotted calves are usually born from early May onwards. The Sika Deer is fairly distinctive and distinguished from Fallow Deer (p. 178) by its antlers, rather 'frowning' expression, short tail, and lack of black on the rump patch; from Red Deer (p. 184) by its small size and spotting, though hybrids occur; and from Roe Deer (p. 192) by its antler shape, and spotted back.

winter

hind

stag

181

WHITE-TAILED DEER
Odocoileus virginianus

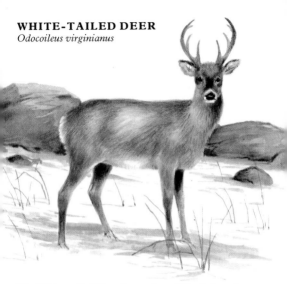

The White-tailed Deer is a native of North America which was introduced into Finland in the 1930s where it is now well established. Males grow to about 1m at the shoulder, with a length of about 2m and a weight of up to 150kg; females are slightly smaller. The most characteristic feature is the white rump and underside of tail, which is wagged back and forth as the animal disappears. White-tailed Deer make a 'whistling snort' when they scent an intruder.

CHITAL *Cervus axis*

The Chital (also known as the Spotted Deer or Axis Deer) is a native of India and Sri Lanka, that has been introduced into northern Yugoslavia, near the Italian border. They stand about 90cm at the shoulder and weigh up to 85kg. It is one of the most beautifully marked of all deer with a reddish brown coat which is thickly spotted at all ages and all times of the year. They are most likely to be confused with Fallow Deer (p. 178).

RED DEER *Cervus elaphus*

The Red Deer is a widespread and often locally abundant deer in many parts of Europe; it is primarily a woodland species but it also occurs in open mountain and moorland habitats. They are rather variable in size – those from the open moorlands being much smaller than those from the southern and eastern woodlands; the weight of a Scottish stag averages 80kg, in the Carpathians over 300kg. A stag

stag

× ¼

forefeet

hind feet

measures up to 250cm in length, and up to 150cm at the shoulder; the females (hinds) are smaller. Both sexes are reddish brown in summer, greyer in winter; the young (calves) are heavily spotted and are born in early summer. During the rut in October males utter loud roars; at other times both deer are usually silent and the sexes live in separate herds. In the winter Red Deer often huddle in sheltered clearings, leaving heavily trampled patches. The droppings are about 20mm long; those of females are elliptical, the males' blunt at one end except during the rut when the droppings are like tiny cow pats. Red Deer are distinguished from Elk (p. 186) by size and head shape.

hind and calf

ELK *Alces alces*

cow

calf

bull

×⅕

foot-
print
in soft
ground

The Elk (known as Moose in North America) is found throughout the northern forests from Scandinavia eastwards to Siberia, Manchuria and Mongolia and south to Poland and Czechoslovakia; in recent years, however, its range has been spreading south and westwards. They inhabit a wide variety of wooded habitats usually with thick undergrowth. The Elk is the largest of all the deer: males (bulls) grow to over 2m at the shoulder, with a maximum length of over 2.5m and a weight of 450kg; the females are smaller. They are very dark coloured with distinctive muzzles and the males have large flat antlers. They are rather shy and, although they may form small mixed herds in winter, they usually lead a solitary life often near rivers or in swampy forests, where they wade and may swim to feed on willows, sallows and other waterside vegetation. During the rut in September the bulls make repeated low grunting and roaring sounds; the males do not form harems. The 1–3 young (usually twins) are born in May or June and accompany the cow until the following spring but do not become sexually mature until they are nearly 3 years old. The Elk is most likely to be confused with the Red Deer (p. 184) which is smaller with a smaller muzzle and has high branching antlers, or with the Reindeer (p. 188) which is smaller, and both sexes of which carry unflattened antlers.

187

REINDEER *Rangifer tarandus*

female

male

×⅙
fore-
feet

hind
feet

reindeer
moss

The Reindeer (known as Caribou in North America) was once found throughout the far north of Europe, and also eastwards through Siberia and to North America and Greenland. It is confined to the tundra zones, and also the more open parts of the taiga, but it is now rare, being extinct in Norway and Sweden and endangered in Finland; it occurs on many Arctic islands, and has been introduced to Iceland and the Cairngorms in Scotland. Reindeer have been domesticated by the Lapps of northern Scandinavia – the domesticated forms are smaller, but otherwise identical. Males stand up to 120cm at the shoulder, are up to 215cm long and weigh up to 150kg; females are slightly smaller. Unlike other deer, both sexes carry antlers, which have large branches over the brow; the female's antlers are smaller. Reindeer live in large herds, of females and young, led by an old female, and smaller herds of males. During the rut the males form harems; the male's voice during the rut is a loud, repeated grunt. Reindeer are not likely to be confused with any other species except possibly the much larger Elk (p. 186).

CHINESE WATER DEER
Hydropotes inermis

The Chinese Water Deer was originally found in the Far East in a small area in the Lower Yangtze Basin, and Korea; it has been introduced into England and France. As its name suggests, in China it is found in wet habitats, but in England it is found in quite dry woodland; it has also recently spread to East Anglia where it is found in wetter areas. The Chinese Water Deer is a small species, about 60cm high at the shoulder and a little under 1m in total length; it weighs up to 16kg. The most distinctive features, apart from the small size, are the lack of antlers, and the tusks, which are clearly visible in the male. It is mainly active by day, and lives a largely

droppings

×½

solitary life; when running it has a rather bounding, rabbit-like gait. It feeds on grasses and herbs and also vegetables, roots and tubers, which it digs up with its tusks. The rut is in December, when the male makes a whistling call and marks his territory with a distinctive musky scent. The fawns are born in late spring or early summer; unlike most deer, twins and triplets are normal, and 4, 5 or 6 young are not uncommon. The adult's footprints are distinctively long and pointed, and when walking the prints are almost perfectly registered, about 35cm apart; at a gallop, the dew claws can be seen in the groups of 4 prints. The droppings are up to 50mm long and rather elongated and deposited in small heaps. It may be confused with the Muntjac (p. 176) which is slightly larger with a hunch-backed appearance, has small antlers (male), white on the tail and more pointed ears.

male, showing tusks

ROE DEER *Capreolus capreolus*

kid
6 weeks
old

doe,
winter

buck, summer, fraying

The Roe Deer is widespread throughout most of
Europe including Britain and Scandinavia; it is absent from most islands, including Ireland. It is found
mainly in woodlands with dense undercover, and
also in more open habitats such as arable land with
hedgerows and copses. It is Europe's smallest native

$\times \frac{1}{3}$

fore-feet

hind feet

droppings

deer, standing up to 75cm at the shoulder and with a length of up to 135cm and weight of about 16kg; the does are smaller. In summer they are reddish brown, in winter greyish brown, with a conspicuous white rump tuft. The antlers of the stag are short and branched. Roe Deer are active by day and night; they emit a loud bark, and when running away, jump well; the male also barks during the rut. The male frays small shrubs and trees and even large herbage during the summer, and the rut starts in late summer. Other signs, such as the 'scrapes' made by bucks and 'rutting rings' where the buck has chased the doe, can sometimes be seen; the droppings are oval, black and 15–20mm long. The heavily spotted kids (often twins) are born in late spring or early summer, and are completely independent by late autumn. Roe Deer are most likely to be confused with the small exotic deer which have been introduced into Europe: the Muntjac (p. 176), Chinese Water Deer (p. 190) and Sika Deer (p. 180).

antlers

1st year

3rd year

4th year

5th/6th year

old, deformed

SAIGA *Saiga tatarica*

migrating group in winter pelage

male, summer

The Saiga antelope was once found throughout the steppes of central Asia, from the Ukraine eastwards through Turkestan to Mongolia and western China. By the 1920s it was reduced to a few isolated populations in the Soviet Union and Mongolia and endangered with extinction. Under strict protection it has increased dramatically and is one of the outstanding conservation success stories; it has recolonised much of its former territory and now numbers hundreds of thousands; it may eventually recolonise parts of the western USSR where suitable habitat exists, although at present it is still absent from European USSR. The Saiga stands about 80cm at the shoulder, is up to 135cm long and weighs up to 45kg. The Saiga is the only true antelope to occur in Europe and the male has lyre-shaped horns (which unlike those of deer are not shed each year). The most distinctive feature of both sexes is the swollen, trunk-like snout, which is an adaptation for breathing in the dust-laden atmosphere of the steppes and semi-deserts in which it lives. The winter coat is much thicker than the short summer fur. Saiga are very gregarious, forming large herds. In spring the sexes separate, but come together for the autumn migrations southwards when the herds can stretch for several kilometres. The voice is a rather sheep-like bleat. One, or occasionally 2 kids are born in spring, and the young become independent at about 6 months old and are sexually mature in their third year. The Saiga is unlikely to be confused with any other species within its European range.

CATTLE

White Cattle

The original wild **Cattle** of Europe, the Aurochs or Urus *Bos taurus*, became extinct in the 17th century; the last is believed to have been killed in Poland in 1627. Several primitive and, until recently, semi-wild herds existed, notably in the United Kingdom. Of these British 'wild' cattle, those at Chillingham in north-east England are the purest and live under the most natural conditions; other herds (some of which have been moved from their original homes to parks and zoos) include those at Dynevor, Chartley, Cadzow and Vaynol in Britain. Primitive cattle similar to British White Cattle exist in several parts of Europe, notably Italy and Hungary. By cross-breeding primitive breeds of cattle, including the long-haired and long-horned British Highland cattle and the Hungarian plains cattle, the extinct Aurochs has been 'reconstructed' and a semi-wild herd now lives in Poland. Herds of primitive cattle also live in a semi-wild state in the Camargue in southern France and Cote Doñana in Spain where they are used as fighting bulls.

The **Water Buffalo** *Bubalis bubalis* is not a native European species but is locally common and domesticated in parts of southern Europe including Italy, Greece, Romania, Bulgaria, Yugoslavia and Hungary. They are distinguished from cattle by their dark colour and flattened backward curving horns. They frequently wallow and wade in water and are often left in a semi-wild state in marshy and coastal areas.

Water Buffalo

EUROPEAN BISON   *Bison bonasus*

The Bison or Wisent was once widely distributed in the woodlands and forests of Europe, but became extinct in the wild in the 1920s; however, there were sufficient numbers in captivity to rebuild a herd in the Bialowieza Forest in Poland and small herds have also been started in the USSR, Romania and elsewhere. The Bison is the largest European land animal and is unmistakable: males stand up to 180cm at the shoulder, are 270cm long and weigh up to 850kg; the cows are smaller. Cows and calves live in small herds and are joined by the bulls during the rut in late summer when the bulls mark their territory by gouging the soil and trees with their horns. The single calf is born in early summer and weaned by autumn. Bison are mainly browsers.

MUSK OX *Ovibos moschatus*

The Musk Ox, which is in fact more closely related to sheep, is a native of North America and Greenland, that has been introduced into Spitzbergen and Dovre Fjell in Norway. It is a large animal, standing up to 165cm at the shoulder, is up to 245cm long and weighs up to 400kg; the females are much smaller than the males. It has a long shaggy coat and the male has characteristic curving horns. Musk Ox live in small herds, which band together in the winter to form large, dense herds. When threatened, they form a defensive circle. The males utter a bellowing call, the young have a sheep-like bleat. The only other large animal in its range is the Reindeer (p. 188) which has antlers and much shorter hair.

CHAMOIS   *Rupicapra rupicapra*

adult male,
winter

The Chamois is found in alpine woodlands, and also above the treeline, in a number of the mountain ranges in Europe, but the populations are all rather fragmented and isolated from each other. The Chamois is goat-like in general appearance, but the horns are rather small and slender, and sharply curved at the end. It grows to a length of up to 130cm, stands up to 80cm at the shoulder, and weighs up to 50kg; the females are much lighter in build. Chamois live in flocks, the males usually separately, though 1 or 2 may accompany the female and young. The

$\times \frac{1}{3}$

ore, walking

ind, leaping

droppings

mating season or rut is from October to December, when the males emit a deep rumbling bleat and there is a great deal of chasing between them; at this time the flocks are mixed. The young (lambs) are born in spring or early summer. When alarmed Chamois make whistling calls; they are very agile and are often seen on very precipitous mountain sides, and like Ibex should be looked for on distant skylines. Chamois may be confused with Ibex (p. 202), which have much more massive horns and lack the head markings, or Roe Deer (p. 192), which are more reddish.

adult male, summer

IBEX AND WILD GOAT

Spanish Ibex

Both species of ibex found in Europe, the **Ibex** or **Steinbok** (*Capra ibex*) and the **Spanish Ibex** (*C. pyrenaicus*), were nearly exterminated during the last century. However, with protection they have recovered and have been introduced into parts of their former range: the Ibex to various parts of the

Alps and the Spanish Ibex to mountainous areas of Spain. Both species are usually found in remote craggy habitats but often descend to lower altitudes during winter. Ibex grow to a length of nearly 1.5m, stand up to 85cm at the shoulder, and weigh up to 55kg; Spanish Ibex are slightly smaller. Both sexes have curving horns but those of the female are smaller and more slender. The sexes live separately for most of the year, in flocks of up to about 20–30 animals. The rut is in midwinter and the 1 or 2 kids are born in late spring or early summer. Within their range Ibex are most likely to be confused with Chamois (p. 200) while domestic sheep and goats are longer haired and rarely have such massive horns.

Wild Goat *C. aegagrus*. This ancestor of the domestic goat is found on Crete and a few other islands in the Aegean. Feral goats occur in various parts of Europe.

×⅓

fore

hind

all
adult
males

Wild Goat

WILD SHEEP

Mouflon

ram

ewe

The Mouflon or Wild Sheep *(Ovis ammon)* is the ancestor of the domestic sheep and is found in many of the more mountainous parts of Asia, and in Europe on the islands of Corsica and Sardinia in mountain forests above the treeline; it has also been introduced into mainland Europe in a variety of deciduous and mixed woodlands and forests, but it prefers dry habitats. The Mouflon is a smallish sheep, growing to about 130cm long and standing up to 75cm at the shoulder; it weighs between 25 and 50kg. Mouflon lack the woolly fleece of domestic sheep; they are

×⅓
fore

hind

brown above, pale below. Males usually have a characteristic pale patch on the flanks (saddle). Rams (males) have well-developed spiral horns; ewes (females) are hornless or have small decurved horns. The rut is in late autumn, when the males often fight; young males play-fight at all times of the year. The single lamb, born in spring, is independent at about 6 months. Mouflon live in small flocks led by an old ewe; non-breeding males live in bachelor flocks. They are active by day and night, and feed mainly on herbs and grasses. The voice is a goat-like bleat.

Soay Sheep *Ovis* domesticated. This is a primitive domesticated sheep, originally from the island of Soay, in St Kilda, Hebrides.

Soay Sheep

WHALES, PORPOISE AND DOLPHINS

Introduction

Although superficially fish-like, whales, dolphins and porpoises (Cetecea) are air-breathing mammals. They all have a blow hole on top of the head, front limbs modified into paddles and rear limbs as a horizontal fluke; some have a dorsal fin but none has the anal fins or gills of fish. The Cetecea fall into 2 groups: the **Toothed whales**, some of which have only vestigial teeth, and the **Baleen whales** which instead of teeth have heavy plates to strain the small fish and invertebrates on which they feed from the water. The shape of the head, the shape and position of the dorsal fin and the size, shape and direction of the vapour cloud produced when the whale 'blows' are important recognition features; in Toothed whales the colour and pattern are often distinctive. Some species 'porpoise' along the surface with the back clear of the water; others 'pitchpole', swimming vertically with the head and part of the body clear of the water. 'Bow-riding' is characteristic of many dolphins; some of the larger species 'breach', leaping clear of the water, and falling back, often with a considerable splash. Toothed whales and occasionally Baleen whales are stranded on European shores; if you find one report it to a natural history museum as soon as possible, or in the United Kingdom to the local coast guards.

KILLER AND BELUGA WHALES

adult
head

female

male

Killer Whale

Beluga Whale

The **Killer Whale** *Orcinus orca*, also known as the Orca Whale, is found off most European coasts including the western Mediterranean but is most frequently observed in the Atlantic and the North Sea. It is the largest member of the dolphin family and the males grow to over 9m, the females slightly less; both sexes bear the distinctive fin which is larger than any other whale's and grows up to 1.8m long in the male. Killer Whales are basically black, with a large proportion of white on the underside, a pale patch on the flanks behind the fin and a white patch on the side of the head; in young animals these patches may be tan or yellowish. Killer Whales are fast-swimming (up to 25 knots), and often travel in groups of up to 30 individuals. They often 'porpoise' and 'pitchpole' – hanging vertically with the fore-parts out of the water. Killer Whales are most likely to be confused with the False Killer (p. 220) and Risso's Dolphin (p. 233).

The **Beluga Whale** *Delphinapterus leucas*, also known as the White Whale, has a circumpolar distribution and, in Europe, is found as far south as Iceland, Arctic USSR and Norway; in cold winters it turns up further south and has been recorded in Danish waters, the Baltic and off the Faeroes, Britain and France. Belugas grow to just under 5m and are almost pure white; young animals are brown and gradually lighten to slate grey and then to pure white after about 7 years. They are heavily built with a distinct neck and smallish head but lack a dorsal fin. Beluga Whales are unlikely to be confused with any other whale.

FIN, BLUE AND SEI WHALES

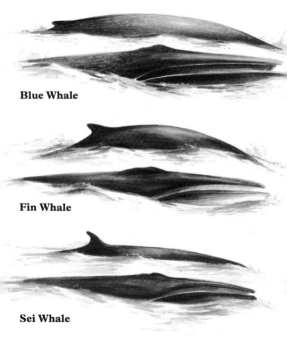

Blue Whale

Fin Whale

Sei Whale

Although much reduced, the **Fin Whale** or **Common Rorqual** *Balaenoptera physalus* is the commonest and most widespread of the great whales in European waters; it occurs in deep waters as far north as the Pacific and has been recorded in the Baltic and Mediterranean; it sometimes comes close to land. It grows to about 25m, and has a dark grey or brownish back and sides, a white belly, and white undersides to the flippers and flukes; the right lower jaw and the front baleen plates are white, those on the left grey. Fin Whales usually live in schools of up to 10 animals; they rarely leap clear of the water. They may be confused with Blue or Sei Whales (see below).

The **Blue Whale** *B. musculus* was once widespread in European waters but is now very rare; it may occasionally be seen off the coasts of Britain, Ireland, Iceland, the Faeroes and Norway. It is the largest living animal, growing to a maxumum length of over 30m, but more usually up to 25m. Its upperside is blue-grey, often with pale spots, its dorsal fin very small and set well back, and the baleen is all black. It may be confused with other species on this page.

The **Sei Whale** (pronounced say) *B. borealis* is a summer visitor to western Europe and is one of the most abundant and widespread of the great whales. It grows to a maximum of about 19m and is similar to the Fin Whale but can be distinguished by its very sharply pointed fin, smaller blow and its habit of rising to the surface at a shallow angle so that the fin can often be seen at the same time as the head.

RIGHT AND GREENLAND WHALES

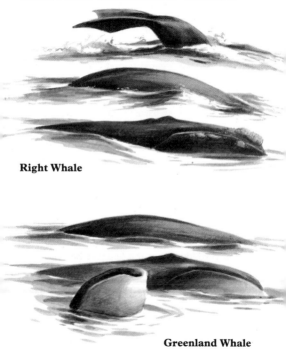

Right Whale

Greenland Whale

The **Right Whale** *Balaena glacialis*, also called the Biscayan Whale, was formerly widespread between 30° and 60°N but is now very rare; it has been recorded from most European waters, including the western Mediterranean and Baltic. It was one of the first whales to be hunted commercially (hence the 'right' whale to kill) and its rarity is a direct result of over-hunting. Right Whales grow to 18m and are completely black with a series of lumps on the top of the head, the 'bonnet'. Other characteristic features included a strongly arched mouth, widely spaced nostrils set far back on the head and forming two distinct upward spouts, a smooth back which lacks fur and bumps, and tail flukes pointed at the tips and concave at the centre; when this whale is swimming on the surface with the mouth open, the baleen appears yellowish grey. The Right Whale is most likely to be confused with the Greenland Whale, or the Sperm or Humpback Whales (p. 214), which have different shaped tails and are variously paler.

The **Greenland Whale** *Balaena mysticetus*, also known as the Bowhead Whale, was at one time widespread north of 64°N but it has been hunted to the brink of extinction. It grows to nearly 20m and is heavily built with a high arching mouth. It often hangs vertically in the water exposing its black head and white or greyish chin. Although their ranges do not normally overlap, the Greenland Whale can be distinguished from the Right by its pale chin and lack of a 'bonnet'; they differ from all other large whales by their arching mouth and lack of a dorsal fin.

HUMPBACK AND SPERM WHALES

Humpback Whale

Sperm Whale

The **Humpback Whale** *Megaptera novaeangliae* was formerly widely distributed in European waters but is now rare due to over-hunting by commercial whalers. In summer it is found in coastal waters off Greenland, Iceland, Spitzbergen and Norway; in winter it migrates southwards. It grows to about 16m, with rather large flippers (up to one third of the body length), a small dorsal fin of variable shape approximately two thirds down the back, and a tall (to 3m), balloon-shaped blow; the head is covered in bumps and the edges of the whitish flippers are scalloped. The Humpback Whale characteristically 'breaches', slaps its tail loudly, and rests on its side with a flipper in the air. At a distance it may be confused with any other great whale but it can be distinguished by its habit of raising the tail high in the air before diving; its blow and very long flippers distinguish it from the Sperm Whale.

The **Sperm Whale** or Cachalot *Physeter catodon* is widely distributed throughout the oceans, particularly in warmer waters, and occurs widely in European waters; it has been stranded on most coasts. It is the largest of the Toothed whales; the male grows to over 20m, the female to usually less than 11m. With its enormous head (up to one third of the total length) and squarish snout which projects well beyond the narrow jaw, it is a distinctive species; in good conditions, it can be identified by its small, compact blow which emerges at a sharp angle from the blow hole on the left front of the head.

RARE WHALES

Pygmy Sperm Whale

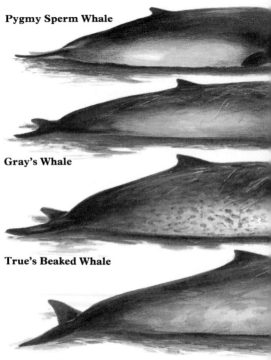

Gray's Whale

True's Beaked Whale

Dense-beaked Whale

RARE WHALES

Pygmy Sperm Whale *Kogia breviceps*. This whale is rarely seen at sea and its range hardly known; there have been a handful of strandings in Europe. The Pygmy Sperm Whale grows to about 3.4m in length and is best identified by its robust build, squarish head and narrow lower jaw; just in front of the flippers is a crescent-shaped mark known as the false gill; unlike the Sperm Whale it has a dorsal fin which is small and located well back. It is usually dark grey on the back and paler on the underside. The Pygmy Sperm Whale is unlikely to be confused with other species in European waters if it is seen at close range.

Gray's Whale *Mesoplodon grayi*. This is the rarest of the Beaked whales found in European waters as a vagrant; its normal range is probably in the Southern Ocean. Little is known about this species and positive identification in the field is impossible, even for stranded specimens, as it is necessary to examine the skull. Gray's Whale grows to a maximum of about 4.6m and is said to be lighter in colour than its closest relative, Sowerby's Beaked Whale (p. 220). The male has 2 onion-shaped teeth in the lower jaw placed further forward; there are 17–22 small teeth in the upper jaw.

True's Beaked Whale *Mesoplodon mirus*. This is another species about which little is known. Its distribution is known mainly from strandings; it has been found stranded on the coast of western Europe and it appears to be a temperate water species. True's Beaked Whale grows to nearly 5m and is rather stout in the mid-body, tapering rapidly towards the tail; the flippers are small, the flukes broad. These whales are dark grey or blackish above, grey on the sides and paler below, and are often covered with blotches and scars. It is most likely to be confused with Cuvier's Beaked Whale (p. 224) which is larger.

Dense-beaked Whale *Mesoplodon densirostris*. Also known as Blainville's Whale, this species is found in tropical and warm temperate waters and is likely to turn up at some stage in European waters. Dense-beaked Whales grow to over 5m and have a rather spindle-shaped body. The most characteristic feature is the head shape, especially the arching contour of the mouth, which makes this species unlikely to be confused with any other Beaked whale at close quarters. Like other Beaked whales they are often scarred. Very little is known about the Beaked whales and it is therefore worth recording every detail observed in the field for any species tentatively identified as a Beaked whale as this may well lead to new discoveries.

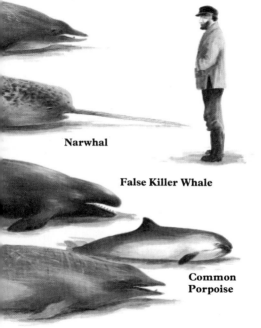

Sowerby's Beaked Whale

Narwhal

False Killer Whale

Common
Porpoise

Gervais' Beaked Whale

221

SMALL WHALES AND PORPOISE

Sowerby's Beaked Whale *Mesoplodon bidens*. This is one of the more widespread of the beaked whales in European waters, particularly the North Sea. It grows to about 5m and has a distinctly spindle-shaped body, tapering at either end. The head has a noticeable bulge in front of the blow-hole, and a slightly concave forehead; the flippers are fairly long. Like other beaked whales they are often scarred. They may occur in small schools of up to 25, but little is known of their behaviour. They may be confused with other Beaked whales.

Narwhal *Monodon monoceros*. This circumpolar species is only occasionally abundant outside Arctic waters. It grows to nearly 5m and the male has a distinctive single spiral tusk (occasionally 2) which grows to a length of up to 2.7m. Apart from this tusk, the Narwhal can be recognised by its mottled grey coloration, the absence of a dorsal fin and a series of bumps about 50mm high along the rear of the body – these can be seen clearly when the animal is swimming on the surface. The only other whale of a similar size found within its range is the very distinctive Beluga (p. 208).

False Killer Whale *Pseudorca crassidens*. Although widespread, these whales have only been infrequently stranded in Europe and are only rarely seen in coastal waters. They grow to a maximum of about 5.5m, are of slender build and are entirely black, except for a grey patch on the belly between the flippers. False Killer Whales are often found in very large herds of 100 or more, and when strandings do occur, large numbers of animals may be involved. They often 'porpoise' and breach and they may ride the bow waves of ships. They are most likely to be confused with the Killer Whale (p. 208) or the Pilot Whale (p. 224).

Common Porpoise *Phocoena phocoena*. Also known as the Harbour Porpoise, this is one of the most frequently observed European whales. It is largely a coastal species and is often found in fjords, sea lochs, bays and rivers; it also occurs in the Black Sea (but is probably extinct in the Mediterranean). It is the smallest European whale, growing to about 1.5m; it is easily identified by its small chunky build and its dark back, lighter sides and almost white belly. Its head is small and the dorsal fin is small and triangular. Common Porpoises are usually found in pairs or groups of up to 10, but they occasionally travel in schools of 100 or more. They often swim at the surface with a characteristic 'porpoising' action. They are unlikely to be confused with any other whale if they are seen at close quarters.

Gervais' Beaked Whale *Mesoplodon europaeus*. Also known as the Antillean Beaked Whale, this is a rare vagrant to European waters from the warm waters of the western Atlantic and Caribbean. It is very similar to other Beaked whales and grows to about 6.7m; it is rather slender with small flippers.

Pilot Whale

Cuvier's Beaked Whale

224

Bottle-nosed Whale

Minke Whale

225

MEDIUM-SIZED WHALES

Pilot Whale *Globicephala melaena*. Also known as Blackfish, Pothead or Caa'ing Whale, this species is widespread and often common in the northern Atlantic and most European waters except the Baltic; it is especially common off the coasts of Scotland, the Scottish Islands and the Faeroes. The Pilot Whale, which grows to just over 6m, can be recognised by its bulbous head, its long sickle-shaped flippers (up to one fifth of the total length) and its distinctive dorsal fin; the fin is set relatively far forward and is low with a long base. These whales may be seen in herds numbering 200 or more but often less than 50; they often 'pitchpole', ie swim with the body vertical and half clear of the water. The Pilot Whale may be confused with the False Killer Whale (p. 220) which has a more slender tapering head and is generally less robust.

Cuvier's Beaked Whale *Ziphius cavirostris*. Little is known about the distribution of this species as they have been only rarely identified at sea and are mainly known from a few strandings. Also known as Goosebeaked Whales, they are the largest of the Beaked whales and grow to around 7m. In stranded specimens the most distinctive features are the indentation at the back of the relatively small head and the small mouth; the dorsal fin is fairly small and set towards the back of the body. These whales are very variable in colour – from dark brown to slate grey or fawn – but the underside and head region are often paler and the body is frequently covered in whitish blotches. Old males have white heads and extensive scarring. Cuvier's Beaked Whales are gregarious and found in schools of 10 to 25; they are difficult to distinguish from other Beaked whales (p. 220–3).

Bottle-nosed Whale *Hyperoodon ampullatus*. This species is found mainly in northern waters and is only occasionally found in the Baltic Sea. The Bottle-nosed Whale is quite large, growing to a maximum length of nearly 10m, and can be recognised by its characteristic bulbous forehead and prominent dolphin-like beak; the beak is often seen clearly as these whales frequently surface to breathe with the head clear of the water. They are usually brownish and may have irregular greyish white heads. They are sometimes found mixed with Atlantic White-sided Dolphins (p. 231) but are most likely to be confused with Beaked whales (pp. 220–6) or the Sperm Whale (p. 241) at a distance.

Minke Whale *Balaenoptera acutorostrata*. This species is also known as the Little Piked Whale or Lesser Rorqual and is found in all oceans and is often locally fairly common. It is the smallest of the Baleen whales, growing to just over 9m, and can be easily identified at close range by the very narrow pointed head, the grey sides and the white band on the flippers; the baleen is yellowish white at the front. They are inquisitive animals and because they frequently approach boats and come close to the shore they are one of the most frequently seen Baleen whales.

Bridled Dolphin

Common Dolphin

Euphrosyne Dolphin

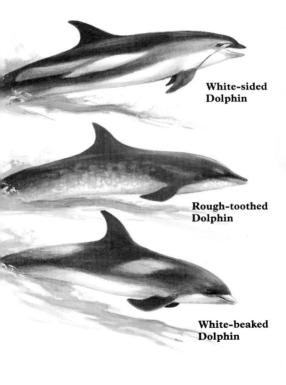

White-sided Dolphin

Rough-toothed Dolphin

White-beaked Dolphin

DOLPHINS

Bridled Dolphin *Stenella frontalis*. Also sometimes known as the Bridled Spotted Dolphin or Cuvier's Dolphin, this is one of the several tropical and subtropical Spotted dolphins which are rarely recorded in European waters. It grows to just over 2m and is best distinguished by the pale sides of the head (the bridle) and the clearly demarcated dark snout.

Common Dolphin *Delphinus delphis*. Also known as the Saddleback Dolphin, this species is widespread in most European waters from southern Norway and Iceland to the Mediterranean and Black Seas; it is occasionally found in the Baltic. It grows to about 2.6m and its distinctive pattern and colour are only likely to be confused with the tropical Spinner Dolphin *S. longirostris* or the Euphrosyne Dolphin (below). They are fast swimming and very active, and are often seen in large schools of up to 1,000+.

Euphrosyne Dolphin *Stenella caeruleoalba*. Also known as the Striped Dolphin, this is a species of warm temperate and tropical waters. It is often the commonest species in the Mediterranean, and is also abundant off the Atlantic coast of Spain, becoming increasingly rare northwards off the coast of France. It has a characteristic thin black line running from the eyes to the flippers and another from the eyes along the sides to the anus, becoming broader at the rear.

White-sided Dolphin *Lagenorhynchus acutus*. This species is widespread in cooler European waters. It is gregarious and often congregates in large schools of up to 1,000, though usually smaller, but does not normally approach ships and ride bow waves. It grows to about 2.7m and has a very distinctive pattern and a tall, broad-based, backward curved fin, a ridge between the fin and rather thick tail and a small but distinct beak.

Rough-toothed Dolphin *Steno bredanensis*. This is a tropical species which has only rarely been recorded in Europe mainly in the Mediterranean and on the Atlantic coasts. It grows to about 2.4m and is characterised by its rather long tapering snout and white lips. They usually form small groups of less than 50 and may ride bow waves.

White-beaked Dolphin *Lagenorhynchus albirostris*. This species is widespread and often abundant in the North Sea and north to Tromso in Norway, Iceland, the Faeroes and south to Britain and Portugal; it is sighted in the Baltic. It grows to just over 3m, has a tall fin, a short beak and 2 pale patches on the dark grey upperparts which are often visible when the animal is swimming and rolling at the surface. They are sociable and may occur in schools of over 500, but are normally found in much smaller schools like those of the White-sided Dolphin (above), with which they may be confused; they do not normally ride the bow wave of boats.

DOLPHINS

Bottle-nosed Dolphin

Risso's Dolphin

Bottle-nosed Dolphin *Tursiops truncatus*. This is one of the most common and widespread dolphins in European waters from the Arctic to the Mediterranean and Black Seas, and often ascends rivers; however, it is rare in the Baltic. They grow to a length of up to about 3.7m, have tall, broad-based dorsal fins, and rather stubby snouts. Bottle-nosed Dolphins are the species most commonly exhibited in zoos and aquaria. The colouring is variable but usually dark grey on the back fading to white on the belly (which may have a pinkish flush). They frequently occur in very large schools and are often playful, riding the bow wave of boats, riding surf and frequently jumping clear of the water. Bottle-nosed Dolphins are most likely to be confused with *Stenella* dolphins (p. 230), the Rough-toothed Dolphin (p. 231) or Risso's Dolphin (below).

Risso's Dolphin *Grampus griseus*. This species is fairly commonly seen around the coasts of western Europe in the Atlantic, North Sea and Mediterranean; less frequently elsewhere. It grows to about 4m and has a very distinctive blunt head and robust body with a tall, pointed dorsal fin. The body colour starts greyish and darkens to almost black with age with pale patches on the belly and chest; old adults are cream or silvery, often with extensive scarring, particularly on the head. Risso's Dolphin is sociable, often travelling in schools of several hundred; they 'porpoise' frequently, and also travel the bow waves of ships. At a distance they are most likely to be confused with Bottle-nosed Dolphins (above).

Index of English Names

Index of Scientific Names

239